The History of

ROGERS'
RANGERS

Volume III

Officers and
Non-Commissioned Officers

BURT GARFIELD LOESCHER

HERITAGE BOOKS
2008

HERITAGE BOOKS

AN IMPRINT OF HERITAGE BOOKS, INC.

Books, CDs, and more—Worldwide

For our listing of thousands of titles see our website
at
www.HeritageBooks.com

Published 2008 by
HERITAGE BOOKS, INC.
Publishing Division
100 Railroad Ave. #104
Westminster, Maryland 21157

Other books by the author:

The History of Rogers' Rangers, Volume I:
The Beginnings, January 1755-April 6, 1758

The History of Rogers' Rangers, Volume II:
Genesis: Rogers' Rangers, The First Green Berets

The History of Rogers' Rangers, Volume IV: The St. Francis Raid

International Standard Book Numbers
Paperbound: 978-0-7884-4751-8
Clothbound: 978-0-7884-1967-6

To
HELENE SUZANNE LOESCHER
This Book
Is Affectionately Dedicated

Contents

All names listed in the highest rank each Officer or non-commissioned man attained in the Corps.

List of Illustrations

—

Preface

To This New Edition

Now that Volumes I and II of *The History Of Rogers' Rangers* are fortunately back in print, it is fitting that Volume III also can take its place along side with them. The first edition of Volume III was very well received, no doubt due to the fact that the names and data of the men who led these famous Rangers in the formative era of our country had never before been made available. The men noted herein were symbolic of the hero wonderment the Rangers presented to their compatriots, the non-Ranger American Provincials. In kind, the Rangers' devotion to Rogers gave him his heroic stature; he returned that devotion to his men, and his renown became theirs.

Consequently it behooved us to issue a new edition of Volume III, now profusely illustrated and with additional discovered data on certain individuals.

As one Rogers' Rangers enthusiast commented: The research cost alone for the data of only one of the individuals documented here would have far exceeded the price for a copy of this, Volume III of *The History Of Rogers' Rangers*. A wise and prudent comment.

The black and white reproductions herein of the author's oil paintings of Rogers' Rangers are in response to the many queries by his readers for a viewing of them. An apology though must be made that they could not have been reproduced in their true color. It is hoped that some day an exhibit of the original 20x24 inch oil paintings (10 to date) may be shown.

An extensive bibliography was not deemed necessary, for the sources are derived from those that built Volume I (primarily the Loudoun and Abercrombie Manuscripts in the Huntington Library) and Volume II (the W.O.34 Amherst Papers). Muster rolls, gleanings from officers' petitions and Ranger officers' correspondence with Rogers, Loudoun, Abercrombie, Wolfe and Amherst were consulted. The LO citations are Loudoun Manuscripts call numbers in the Huntington Library, San Marino, California. The W.O.34 citations may be found in the War Office, 34 Amherst Collection in the Public Records Office, London.

The Rangers' names appear alphabetically by the highest office they attained in Rogers' Rangers. If this is not known, consult the name index in the back of the volume. All mentions of "discharged" are honorable, unless stated otherwise. The name only, of the Rogers' Ranger Company is cited, viz., for the individual's service. Other Regular or Provincial regiments they may have served in are listed by full title or number. It is assumed that the reader is a student of the historical events and personages of the periods involved. Hence, no repetitious description.

The author would like to mention that he has no other genealogical or biographical information on the individuals written on in this book. Other, or additional data is up to the reader.

ROGERS ISLAND opposite Fort Edward on the Hudson River was Rogers' Rangers' base hut-camp from 1755 to 1759. Rocque Collection, Boston Public Library.

ROGERS' RANGERS—GENESIS OF AMERICANISM

An historical discourse delivered by Burt G. Loescher before the Rogers Island Historical Association on September 13, 1969

It is with great pleasure that I stand here at the Rangers' most famous home base to deliver these words on Rogers' Rangers. It is most fitting that Mr. Earl Stott and his Rogers' Island Historical Association enthusiasts should unearth and preserve the remarkable artifacts they have discovered of the Ranger's life. For no matter how complete, or how different the printed concept, there is always another fossil to enhance a recognized fact. That is the utter fascination of the documentary historical research or the archeological quest. For those smitten with the virus of the chase, and the true historians and archeologists are, all other existence pales in comparison.

For us Americans, the adrenaline-stirring arousal induced by Scottish bagpipe wails will never equal the shouts and sounds of Rogers' Rangers as they "flowed and ebbed" from Rogers' Island. It is not hard to close one's eyes for a moment and envision scouts of Rogers' Rangers emerging from the ford between their island and Fort Edward in a splashing, shouting group, not unlike a collection of demons being cast upon the Hudson shore: then again, returning on a later ebb from their various and startling interludes with death, sometimes in the dead of night or pregnant morn, flowing back like so many wild phantoms. It is no wonder that the startled English sentries at Ford Edward stirred anxiously more than once when one of these wild bands flowed by.

Probably no other body of American fighting men has piqued the interest of Americans, English and Canadians, nor maintained their curiosity during the many decades since Rogers' Rangers flowed and ebbed from their various encampments to harry the enemy, and played a vital role in the formative period of our early history. Unlike other famous corps, such as the Texas Rangers and the Royal Canadian Northwest Mounted Police, Rogers' Rangers existed during a most critical and formative period of American-Canadian history. They personified the very best of the colonial fighting men. They were akin to the Grenadier and Light Infantry companies in the English army. This was the case in the colonial eyes, if not those of the English regulars.

A few words on the lack of acceptance of Rogers' Rangers as a superior fighting force, by the English officers and commanders, would not be amiss, for it was this refusal of recognition that actually prolonged the French and Indian War. Unfortunately, the mind of an eighteenth-century English officer lacked the psychological acumen of his followers in the twentieth century. The English commanders-in-chief, Loudoun, Abercrombie and Amherst, new to the terrain and provincial freedom of thought in the American colonies, would not, and could not, accept Rogers' method of "leveling his recruits" into effective Rangers to combat their unique savage foe in his own terrain. It is wondered if the official title given to Rogers' Rangers by the English, viz.: "His Majesty's *Independent* Companies of Rangers," was indeed a fitting descriptive title, because their frequent mentions of Rogers' Rangers in their correspondence and journals are a repetitious diatribe on their concept of the Rangers as an independent-minded body.

The English armies on the various fronts in the French and Indian War would have been irretrievably lost without Rogers' Rangers. The Rangers were the eyes of the various commanders-in-chief, even though they were reluctant to admit it. Nobody likes to admit his dependency upon another, whether it is an individual, or a body of men. The invariable pattern is that of jealousy rather than gratitude, and the adamant English concept of military conduct accentuated the void of understanding between them and the tactics of warfare conducted by Rogers' Rangers. Major Rogers' "Ranging Rules" were the only applicable tactics for the woods warfare conducted in North America. Unfortunately for the early success of English arms in the first half of the war at least, their insistence upon not accepting Rogers' Ranging Rules prolonged their eventual success, which their superior numbers and adequacy of supply should have guaranteed them earlier, if the English commanders had adapted themselves to Ranger tactics.

The catastrophes of the 1758 fiasco against Ticonderoga and Rogers' disastrous losses at Rogers' Rock and in his St. Francis Raid retreat should never have happened. These concepts are revealed in our other volumes on Rogers' Rangers: namely Volume I, *The Beginnings*, which covers the years from 1755 through 1758, and Volume II, titled *Genesis: Rogers' Rangers—The First Green Berets*, their concluding history to the end of the American Revolution. Each volume is complete in itself for the periods covered. A biographical register of all Rogers' Rangers officers and (known) men has been prepared, and a manuscript entitled "*Rogers' St. Francis Raid: Fact, Legend And Lost Treasure*" also was felt necessary due to the wealth of new evidence uncovered by this writer, so that a definitive account of the controversial raid from all sides will be under one cover for posterity.

If one wonders how such an apparent monumental work of Rogers' Rangers was effected, all I can say is that my interest is primarily in Rogers' Rangersana, and memorabilia of them. This interest has been long and steadfast, and my findings in the research chase have been fortunate.

Returning to the paper at hand, Rogers' Rangers were never given the opportunity to exhibit their full potential. The Battle of Ticonderoga could have been avoided if Rogers' 1757 proposal to Loudoun to capture Crown Point had been granted. Instead, his plan was pirated and procrastinated until it degenerated into Rogers being granted a "boon" to make his death march to Rogers' Rock with less than half the Rangers he had asked for.

One of the catastrophes that can be directly linked with omissions and procrastination by the English commanders was the horror of the return march from Rogers' St. Francis Raid. Rogers had a much more feasible plan for the raid years earlier which offered him a much safer approach and return march. His enforced 1759 retreat was a mean reward for all the Yankee grit and determination that, notwithstanding, effected one of the most incredible marches in history.

Still another opportunity to make the most of the unique potential of Rogers' Rangers was dissipated when Rogers wanted to rectify the "incomplete victory" of his St. Francis Raid. Shortly after his return, during that very 1759-1760 winter, he amazed Amherst when he petitioned him to march to the relief of Murray at Quebec with 500 Rangers via the Kennebec River on snowshoes. Although impressed by Rogers' offer, still Amherst did nothing about it. Murray's defeat at Ste. Foye could have been averted with the timely arrival of Rogers' much needed relief force.

Although Rogers' Rangers were never allowed to reach their full potential, still their great moments were in their commando successes at turning points of the war. A few of their highlights which stand forth in history like polished gems were: their protective screen covering Abercrombie's retreat down Lake George after his bloody defeat at Ticonderoga; Rogers' timely defeat of Marin near Fort Anne, which bolstered English morale at a time when the whole Lake George front was in danger of crumbling after the battle of Ticonderoga; the "foreign service" of the companies of Rogers' Rangers at Louisbourg and Quebec; Ranger Ensign Francis Carruthers' heroic landing at Freshwater Cove which enabled Amherst to successfully besiege Louisbourg; the incredible exploits of the company under Captain Moses Hazen at Quebec, particularly their gallant stand at Ste. Foy on Murray's wing, enabling the defeated English army to retire to Quebec, which was never fully credited to them; Rogers' St. Francis Raid as mentioned; Rogers' skillful victory at Pointe au Fer in 1760, which was the most complete success of Rogers' Rangers, due greatly to Ranger Lieutenant Jacob Farrington's brilliant flank maneuver through the swamp (the same Farrington who led the platoon of Rogers' Rangers to success against Great Warrior at Etchoe Pass in the Cherokee-English War); last, but not least, Black Jones' audacious odysseys as a Rogers' King's Ranger Captain in the last Loyalist revival in the Revolutionary War. These and so many, many more, are too numerous to recount at this time, but are set forth in detail in their history mentioned earlier.

Rogers' Rangers were synonymous with the free spirit stirring throughout the American colonies in the mid-eighteenth century, increasing in intensity to the storm of the American Revolution two decades later. As a body of men they, as one of the discerning officers wrote, personified the new breed of free men that so startled the English officers with their Yankee independence. There was a camaraderie with the men that evoked the best from them. They shared the equality of freedom of expression and left a legacy of great men: John Stark, Moses Hazen, the Brewers (Jonathan and David), Joseph Wait—all were great Ranger captains. They were but a few of the Rangers to lead the fight to independence in the Revolution. At the same time, other equally free men, Robert and James Rogers, chose to embrace the Loyalist cause as Rogers' Ranger revivals.

A fraternity of men, whether a regiment, or a nation, must have its heroes, and they become symbols. The Rangers' devotion gave Major Rogers his stature and by so doing he gave it back because his renown became theirs. Unfortunately, their hero was only mortal and he faded. Taking a few ill-chosen trails, he was surpassed by his Rangers.

The epitaph of the Corps might well read:

> *They won Canada from France so that the American Colonies might be free to win their independence from England; and then strove to defend Canada from American occupation so that two great countries might be born. The United States and Canada can both proudly claim ROGERS' RANGERS.*

Burt G. Loescher

MAJOR ROBERT ROGERS
Thom. Hart, London, 1776.

THE LIEUTENANT COLONEL

ROBERT ROGERS:

Nov 7-1731: Born in Methuen, Mass. fourth son of James Rogers, Sr. and Mary McFatridge.

April 1740: The Rogerses move to Lovell's Farm across the N.H. line and 16 miles from Rumford (now Concord, N.H.).

1744-48: Rogers sees action in King George's War when only 15 years old; served as a private in Captain Daniel Ladd's Scouting Company July 16-Oct 2, 1746 that guarded the frontier of N.H. Served in same capacity in Ebenezer Eastman's Scouting Company on the same duty Aug 1-Sept 12, 1747.

1748: Rogerses' Farm destroyed by St. Francis Indians. Only one apple tree of a young orchard survived—and the Rogerses.

1752: Rogers' father, clad in deerskins and bowed by age, is mistaken for a bear and shot by a friend. Rogers is 21.

1753: Rogers starts his adulthood by building a house and barn at Dunbarton, N.H. and locating a tenant while he follows the alluring life of a trapper and trader, roaming as far as Canada.

1754: Aug 23-Sept 21—Rogers serves as a Private in Blanchard's detachment of the N.H. Regiment posted on the Connecticut River.

1755: Jan-Raises 24 N.H. men for Nova Scotia service in Shirley's Massachusetts Regiment.

1755: Feb 7-Arrested on suspicion of counterfeiting printed tender.

1755: Feb 12-Clears himself by breaking his contract with Massachusetts and taking himself and his 24 men into the N.H. service.

1755: April-Commissioned Captain of the first Company of Blanchard's N.H. Regiment designated as a Ranger Company. The Genesis of ROGERS' RANGERS is born.

1755: June-Builds Fort Wentworth at the forks of Connecticut and Upper Ammonoosuc Rivers in Coos County, New Hampshire.

1755: Aug 20-Rogers and his Company are detached from the N.H. Regiment to join Johnson at Lake George and comprise his scouting arm.

1755-1761: Rogers takes detachments of his battalion of Rangers into 27 recorded battles and scouts during the French and Indian War into the heart of French Canada.

1761: Feb 14-Arrives at N.Y. from Detroit Expedition and Amherst rewards him with the Captaincy of Paul Demere's S.C. Independent Company of Regulars. Rogers' commission dated from Oct 25, 1760.

1761: June 30-Marries Elizabeth Browne, daughter of Reverend Arthur Browne, Portsmouth, N.H. She is 20 and Rogers is 29.

1765: June-While seeking favor in high London circles Rogers enhances his fame. His coach is held up by a highwayman and while reaching into the window to demand the Ranger's wallet, Rogers pulls him into the coach with one arm and collects the reward.

1765: Aug 12-Rogers presents a memorial to the King's Council urging a search for the Northwest Passage.

1765: Oct-His *Journals* and *Concise Account Of North America* are published by John Millan in London, after taking only three months to write them. He is appointed "Governor" of Michilimackinac.

1765: Dec-Rogers completes his play, *Ponteach.*

1765: Dec 18-Rogers sails for America on the frigate *Resolute.*

1766: Jan 15-Arrives in N.Y. Gage reluctantly hands him his commission and instructions for Michilimackinac, June 10.

1766: July 23-Figures prominently in Johnson's huge Indian Conference at Oswego (while on his way to

Michilimackinac) attended by Pontiac and the Northwestern tribes.

1766: Aug-Arrives at Michilimackinac with wife, Elizabeth, and Nathaniel Potter, his secretary.

1766: Sept 12-Sends J. Tute towards the Mississippi to map the country in preparation for Rogers' anticipated order to seek the Northwest Passage.

1767: June 23-Benjamin Roberts arrives at Michilimackinac to supervise the Indian trade. Clashes with Rogers over rum withdrawals. Rogers send him to Gage on an insubordination charge.

1767: Dec-Gage orders Rogers confined in irons at Michilimackinac through the winter hoping that he will die before spring and he can be sent to Montreal to face a trumped-up charge of treason.

1768: June-Arrives at Montreal for trial, held from Oct 12-31, court-martialed and acquitted.

1769: June-Sails for London. Receives an audience with George III and taps the Royal Treasury for 3,000 pounds sterling but his drive for a baronetcy and a pension fails. Brings suit against Gage for assault and imprisonment.

1770: June-His creditors close in and he is thrown into Fleet Prison in London.

1770: Sept 29-Petitions George III for a commission in the East India Company, enclosing favorable recommendations from past military commanders and associates. His petition is rejected.

1772: Feb 11-Again petitions the King from Fleet Prison-this time a repeated petition to discover Northwest Passage.

1773: June-Rescued from prison by brother James who gives bond for his debts.

July 1773-March 1775: Claims to be serving as a mercenary soldier for the Bay of Algiers, Africa.

1775: April-Back in London again petitions for an appointment in India — Fails.

June 1775-1783: See Vol. II, *History of Rogers' Rangers*

1783-1795: Apparently spends these closing 12 years of his life in London living improvidently on his half-pay as a retired Captain of the English army.

May 18, 1795: Rogers dies in his 63rd year in poor lodgings. He is buried at St. Mary, Newington in the southern part of London.

THE MAJOR

JAMES ROGERS:

Born in Methuen, Mass. about 1726, the third son of James, Sr. and Mary McFatridge.

Ensign of Hobbs' Nov 17, 1756. First Lieutenant Hobbs' (Bulkeley's) Feb 27, 1757.

Captain of a new Company Jan 14, 1758.

Served the war to Nov 11, 1760.

Outfitted a Privateer, the *Major Rogers* at Charlestown, S.C. in 1761 to prey on Spanish shipping.

Land deeds show that in 1760 and 1761 he owned land in Starkstown, N.H. On May 6, 1760 he purchased land in Londonderry, N.H. and soon moved there. Dec 10, 1762 he conveyed to Robert Rogers of Porstmouth, N.H. land in Suncook (conveyed to James by Abraham Kimball on March 2, 1761).

Married Margaret, daughter of Reverend David McGregor. Children: David, b. Nov 7, 1762, died Nov 2, 1766. James, b. Nov 22, 1764. David, b. about 1771 & 3 daughters.

Moved to Kent, now Londonderry, Vt. in 1774. Showing a tendency to the Loyalist cause his wealthy estates in Vermont were confiscated and he was driven from his wife and five children into Canada.

Commissioned Major June 2, 1779, by General Clinton at N.Y. of Rogers' Rangers & commanded the KING'S RANGERS Battalion for remainder of Revolutionary War.

In 1784, he settled at Fredericksburgh on the Bay of Quinte with a number of his Rangers and here he died in 1792 age 58.

FALCONS OF THE LAKES. Rogers atop Black Mountain,
Vermont, with Capt John Stark in June 1756, looking for secret
passage to Ticonderoga. Another 20x24 inch oil painting by
Burt Loescher of "Historic Moments of Rogers' Rangers."

THE CAPTAINS

DAVID BREWER: 22nd Captain
Of Sudbury, Mass.

First Lieutenant of Moses Brewer's before May 11, 1759, and stationed at Stillwater with a platoon. Ordered by Amherst on May 11, 1759 to recruit for a new Company and to be commissioned the Captain when Company was recruited. Could not raise more than a platoon and though not commissioned Captain commanded this distinct Company and was posted at Fort George for remainder of 1759 campaign. Commissioned Captain in spring of 1760 when he completed his Company.

Settled on his War Land Grant. In American Revolution, commissioned Colonel of the 12th Massachusetts Regiment of Continentals on June 17, 1775. Stationed at Roxbury he and his Regiment figured conspicuously in Siege of Boston. Cashiered Oct 24, 1775 or in 1780 after a court-martial. (Conflicting dates offered by Heitman's Registrar and H. Sewell's Journal at Ticonderoga.)

JONATHAN BREWER: 11th Captain
Of _____, Mass.

Ensign in Shirley's Massachusetts Regiment in Nova Scotia in 1755. Led brilliant winter scouts against enemy during 1755-6 winter in Nova Scotia.

Commissioned Ensign in Speakman's Nov 17, 1756. First Lieutenant of John Stark's Feb 24, 1757 replacing S. Kennedy killed Jan 21. Captain of a new Company Jan 14, 1758. Served the War to Nov 11, 1760.

Of Waltham, Mass. at time of Revolution. Colonel of a Massachusetts Regiment at Bunker Hill.

A close associate and advisor of General George Washington.

MOSES BREWER: 13th Captain

Of Massachusetts

In Provincial service in Nova Scotia in 1757. Recommended by Rogers for the Captaincy of a proposed Connecticut Mohegan Indian Company of Rogers' Rangers on Jan 10-11, 1758. Commissioned Captain by Loudoun on Jan 14, 1758. Resigned Nov 24, 1759.

CHARLES BULKELEY: 7th Captain

Of Littleton, Mass.

Lieutenant in Phineas Osgood's Company of Shirley's Massachusetts Provinical Regiment in 1755 in Nova Scotia campaign.

First Lieutenant of Hobbs' Sept 1, 1756 (on Aug 1, 1756 roll). Captain of Hobbs' April 25, 1757. Killed March 13, 1758 at Battle of Rogers' Rock.

JONATHAN BURBANK: 16th Captain

Of New Hopkinton, N.H.

Captured by St. Francis Indians at garrison house there on April 22, 1746. Later taken captive to Montreal where he was later redeemed.

Entered Rogers' Own Company June 1, 1756 as Sergeant. Ensign same Company July 23, 1756. Second Lieutenant J. Stark's Feb 26, 1757, First Lieutenant Rogers' Own Jan 14, 1758. Captain of Bulkeley's April 7, 1758.

Massacred by Indians who mistook him for Rogers on May 11, 1759 at ruins of Fort William Henry. When his death was confirmed by exchanged Ranger prisoners, his wife Ruth had the following notice printed in the *New Hampshire Gazette,* Jan 11, 1760: "All Persons that have any just Demands on the Estate of Capt. Jonathan Burbank, late of New Hopkinton..., deceased, are desired to bring in their accounts to Ruth Burbank...aforesaid Administratrix of said Estate: and all who are indebted to said Estate are desired to make speedy Payment or to renew their Bonds, to prevent further trouble. Dec 27, 1760."

JACOB CHEEKSAUNKUN: 2nd Captain
Of Stockbridge, Mass. War Chief of the Stockbridge Mohegan Indians.

Originally recruited by William Johnson to serve with him against Crown Point in 1755 in Company of Stockbridges raised by Johnson's henchman, Captain Staates. After their arrival at Albany, Johnson did not include them in his army. However, they accompanied Shirley to Oswego when he passed through and engaged their services. In December 1755, Shirley commissioned Cheeksaunkun to raise a Company of Stockbridges for the 1756 campaign, and commissioned him Captain May 27, 1756. Discharged Nov 11, 1756 by Loudoun.

Re-commissioned Captain Jan 27, 1758. Discharged by Abercrombie on Sept 11, 1758.

Re-commissioned Captain by Amherst, evidently dated March 25, 1759, the date of his conference with Rogers at Albany to reenter Rogers' Rangers. Captured on Lake George July 5, 1759. Endeavoring to escape during winter of 1759-60 he lost his toes when they froze. Released Oct 6, 1760.

MOSES HAZEN: 19th Captain
Born June 1, 1733 at Haverhill, Mass. A tanner by trade.

A Lieutenant in Shirley's Massachusetts Provincial Regiment in Nova Scotia 1755.

Enlisted before April 15, 1756, into Captain Edmund Mooer's Company of Saltonstall's Massachusetts Provincial Regiment as a Lieutenant. At Fort Edward on July 26, and at Fort William Henry, Oct 11, 1756. Served in Kennedy's daring expedition Aug 15-Sept 7, 1756. Kept a detailed *Journal* (LO 1728). States he was left a day's march behind Kennedy's objective with 3 men as a reserve. He querulously adds: "For what reason we were left behind I can't tell for we were all well and in good spirits."

Recommended by Rogers on Jan 10, 1758 for the First Lieutenancy of McCurdy's proposed Company of Rangers. Commissioned Second Lieutenant in that Company by Loudoun on Jan 14, 1758. Refused to accept because it would not give him a promotion. When the First Lieutenant (H. I. Wendell), received a Captaincy of a new Company on April 7, 1758, Hazen re-entered McCurdy's as the First Lieutenant. After McCurdy's death at Fort Frederick, Nova Scotia, Hazen replaced him as Captain—commissioned by Amherst on April 6, 1759. Served the War and discharged Feb 20, 1761. Petitioned Amherst through Appy, his Secretary, from Albany on Nov 19, 1760, to allow him to recruit his Company, rather than have Ogden take the best from its remnants for his Company of Rangers—modestly adding: "...I think according to what little experience I have gained they might do double the service as those Men that are commonly raised." Upon being rejected he purchased a Lieutenancy in the 44th Regiment, dated Feb 21, 1761. On Aug 11, 1761 he petitioned the Secretary of War, asking to be promoted to Captain—to rank from April 6, 1759, the date of his Captain's commission in Rogers' Rangers. At the same time (Aug 8, 1761) General Murray recommended him to Amherst in words that clearly reveal the high regard British officers as well as Provincials held of him: "To whom it may concern—During all that severe 1759-60 winter, Captain Hazen was, from the circumstances of affairs, ever upon duty. He was always ready and willing to go upon every service, even the most hazardous, on the least notice. It would not be doing him Justice if I did not add, that I have had several opportunitys to observe his Behaviour in action, wherein he Discovered, so much skill, Bravery and good Conduct, as would justly entitle him to every military reward he could ask or demand. I wish I could procure him such a one, as I think he deserves." As nothing resulted from his petition, Hazen repeated it to Amherst in late 1762. Amherst replied on Oct 28, 1762: Stating he was aware of his good services. His desire to continue and raise himself in army commendable and that he will provide for him "whenever an opportunity offers." (W.O. 34, 87/92; 94; 93/199) Still no Captaincy forthcoming, Hazen resigned in disgust in 1763, and retired on half-pay. Settling at St. John's, Quebec, he became a prosperous farmer maintaining sawmills, a forage and a potash house. He entered the Catholic Church on Jan 11, 1765. The same day, Governor Murray made Hazen and others, Tribunals of Police of Montreal. In Dec, 1770, Hazen married Charlotte de la Saussaye at Montreal.

When the Revolution broke out Hazen fell under suspicion from both sides. He joined Montgomery and took part in the attack on Quebec and in the Siege of Montreal. After the retreat he spent the winter in Albany, recruiting for the 2nd Canadian Regiment of which he was made Colonel on Jan 22, 1776. The Regiment known as "Congress's Own," he raised partly in Canada and among Canadian refugees. Hazen led the Regiment in the Staten Island Campaign, the battles of Germantown, Brandywine, and the Siege of Yorktown. In the summer of 1779, Hazen was sent to build a military road to the Canadian border. Later he was recalled to N.J. where he was busy trying to collect money for his unpaid Regiment. On June 29, 1781, Congress brevetted him a Brigadier-General. At the close of the war he resigned on Jan 1, 1783 and settled in Vermont with his two brothers where he had bought land during the War.

Hazen died in Troy, N.Y., Feb 3, 1803, seventy years old. (Chase: *History of Haverhill; Recherches Historiques*, III, p 156, VII, 159. The above biographical sketch a source for Dr. Everest's fine biography, *Moses Hazen and the Canadian Rangers*, University of Syracuse Press.)

HUMPHREY HOBBS: 3rd Captain

A Deacon of Souhegan (now Amherst), N.H.

In 1745 he surveyed the roads for the town. Elected Deacon of the Congregational Church Jan 6, 1742. But resigned the following year to enter military service against the French and Indians; becoming famous for his many successful fights with the Indians in King George's War, much to the chagrin of the

Indians, who afterwards said "Souhegan Deacon no very good, He fight Sabba-day." On June 26, 1748, he was leading 40 men from No. 4, N.H., to Fort Shirley, when he was attacked by a large body of Indians. After a four-hour battle the Indians withdrew.

He was a Captain in Winslow's Expedition to build Fort Halifax on the Kennebec in 1754.

In May 1756, raised a Company of Rangers in Boston. Loudoun dated his Captain's commission Sept 1, 1756. Because of his knowledge, not only of the Kennebec River, but the regions about No. 4, N.H., he submitted to Loudoun detailed written accounts of "The River Kennebec" on Sept 17, 1756; and the next day, "An Account of the way from No. 4 to N.H., to the Mouth of Otter Creek."

Succumbed to Smallpox at Fort William Henry and died on Feb 22, 1757. (LO 1824, 1839; Hoyt, *Antiquarian Researches*, Bearce, R.: "Vermont," 1966 edition, p 278 for 6/1748 Battle.)

NOAH JOHNSON: 18th Captain

Born in Dunstable, N.H.

In 1725, he fought in Lovewell's Fight with the Pequots as the First Sergeant of Lovewell's famed Company of Indian fighters.

Of Rumford, N.H. by 1755.

In 1745, served as Private in John Goffe's N.H. Company, scouting and guarding the Bedford, Milford and Derryfield garrisons in King George's War.

A Sergeant in Rogers' First Company of Blanchard's N.H. Regiment from April 24-Oct 6 1755. Acting Sergeant in Rogers' Oct 6-Nov 25, Volunteer Company.

Ensign, Nov 25, 1755 of 55-56 Winter Company. Ensign, March 24, 1756 of Rogers' New Company. First Lieutenant of Richard Rogers' July 24, 1756, but not commissioned until Nov 2, 1756. Served in that capacity until capitulation of Fort William Henry on Aug 9, 1757 and disbandment of Richard Rogers' Company, per terms of surrender. Re-entered Corps in winter of 1758-9, as Captain of Neale's.

Mortally wounded June 5, 1760, at Battle of Point au Fer (shot through the body, head and left arm) and died on board ship while returning to Crown Point for medical aid. Johnson was the eldest Captain in Rogers' Rangers, being between 50-55 years old at the time of his death.

JOHN McCURDY: 9th Captain
Of Dunbarton, N.H. Son of James.

Sergeant in Rogers' original Company, Jan-May to June 6, 1756. Continued as Sergeant until July 24. Second Lieutenant of Rogers' Own, July 24, 1756. First Lieutenant, Feb 24, 1757. Captain of a new Ranger Company, Jan 14, 1758. Served at Siege of Louisbourg and Monckton's St. John's River Raid after Siege. Stationed with Company at Fort Frederic (mouth of St. John's River) where he was killed Jan 30, 1759, while on woodcutting duty—a chopped tree fell on him.

JACOB NAUNAUPHTAUNK: 14th Captain
A Stockbridge Mohegan of Stockbridge, Mass. Son of Jacob Cheeksaunkun.

In 1748 he was elected to the respected office of "Hogreeve" of the town of Stockbridge—vesting him with the power to seize all "wild swine" going without a keeper without yoke or tethering line or means of restraint. (*N.E. Historical Gen. Reg.,* V. 36, p. 273.)

Lieutenant of Jacob Cheeksaunkun's May 27 to Nov 11, 1756. Captain of a Company of Stockbridge Indian Rangers Jan 27, 1758. Discharged by Abercrombie Sept 11, 1758.

Re-commissioned Captain by Amherst March 25, 1759 the date of his agreement with Rogers. Captured with Kennedy in Aug 1759, by a hunting party of St. Francis Indians. Sold to the French who kept him in irons aboard a prison ship at Montreal. Loaned 644 livres by Captain Tute for subsistence while a prisoner. 1760 his release was obtained by Priest Roubaud and he was sent to Amherst arriving at Fort Levis Aug 29. It implied hope for peace with the English. Amherst now sent Jacob as peace envoy to the St. Francis tribe.

JAMES NEALE: 17th Captain

Of Amoskeag, N.H.

From Aug 23-Oct 1, 1755, Captain of a scouting party of N.H. men raised in the summer to guard the frontiers of N.H. First Lieutenant Shepherd's new Company Feb 28, 1757. Abercrombie commissioned him Captain of a new Ranger Company April 7, 1758. Resigned from service during 1758-59 winter.

AMOS OGDEN: 23rd Captain

Of New Jersey.

Captain in the N.J. Provincial Regiment at Oswego in 1756. Had an engagement with the enemy in boats near Portland Point on June 24, 1756. Captain in N.J. "Blues" 56-9.

Commanded the Provincials in Rogers' St. Francis Raid in 1759. Wounded in attack.

His petition to Amherst for a Ranger Company March 1760 was granted and he served with his Company in Amherst's advance on Montreal. Kept in service at end of War and served with his Ranger Company in West Indies campaign, 1761-2. Discharged with his Company in N.Y. about June 16, 1762.

As early as spring of 1759 he had petitioned Gage for a Captaincy in Rogers' Rangers, who recommended him to Amherst on April 9, 1759 for Captaincy of Wendell's. (W.O. 34, 46A/27.)

In 1767 English Privy Council granted him 25,000 acres of land in West Florida. (Acts Privy Council, Colonial, 1766-1783.)

RICHARD ROGERS: 5th Captain

Born in Methuen, Mass, May 6, 1734, 5th son of James Rogers, Sr. and Mary McFatridge.

Sergeant in Captain William Simes' 10th Company of Blanchard's 1755 N.H. Regiment. Served from April 24-Oct 4, 1755.

Acting Lieutenant, Rogers' Volunteer Ranger Company, Oct 4-Nov 28, 1755. Lieutenant of winter Ranger Company, Nov 28, 1755. In same capacity until July 24, 1756, when he was commissioned by Abercrombie, Captain of a new Company of Rogers' Rangers to be raised by him. Succumbed to smallpox and died at Fort William Henry on June 22, 1757.

JOHN SHEPHERD: 8th Captain

Of Canterbury, N.H. Eldest son of Samuel.

Captain in Meserve's N.H. Regiment in 1756. Captured in Aug, 1756 and taken to Montreal. Escaped the middle of Oct 1756.

Met Rogers (while escaping) at Lake George on a scout and returned to Loudoun's camp at Fort Edward with valuable information on the French in Canada. Captain of a new Company of Rogers' Rangers, Feb 25, 1757. Because of poor health he tendered Amherst his resignation on June 25, 1759 and it was accepted on July 12.

During Revolution, settled at Amherst, N.H. and was called the infamous John Shepherd, by the Committee of Safety. In Oct 1776, he deserted from the American Army and went to N.Y., where Rogers gave him a Captain's commission in his Queen's Rangers. Soon after, he was apprehended, with orders sewed in his breeches to enlist Ranger recruits and was committed to jail in Connecticut. He escaped, but was again seized and sent to prison in Exeter, N.H. and though with irons on his hands and feet and chained to the floor, he escaped a second time. His subsequent activities are unknown, for Rogers' Queen's Rangers had undergone a transformation and he was no longer carried as a Captain in the Corps.

THOMAS SPEAKMAN: 4th Captain

Of Boston, Mass.

Captained a Company in Winslow's Battalion of Massachusetts Provincials in Nova Scotia in 1755. Served at capture of Beausejour in 1755 and was instrumental in rounding up the Acadians for deportation; having at one time a desperate beach fight with Boishebert and 300 Acadians and Indians. Served in a winter raid in 1755-6, ordered by Monckton to encircle the head of the bay. Burned 150 houses. On Dec 1, 1755, sailed for Halifax and Boston with Winslow's battalion.

Commissioned by Shirley in May 1756, to raise a Company of Rangers from the Nova Scotia winter garrisons of Massachusetts Provincials returning to Boston. Commissioned Captain of this Company by Loudoun on Sept 1, 1756.

Mortally wounded at Battle of La Barbue (Five Mile) Creek Jan 21, 1757. Scalped alive the next day when he was found by Indians who also decimated his head.

JOHN STARK: 6th Captain

Born at Londonderry, N.H. Aug 28, 1728, 3rd son of Archibald. A companion of the Rogers brothers in his youth. Captured by the St. Francis Indians while on a hunting trip in 1752. By his courage he earned his captors' respect and was well treated, being later redeemed. Engaged in March 1753 by a Provincial Surveying party to guide them in surveying and making a road to Coos. In June 1754 he guided a party under Captain Peter Powers sent by Governor Wentworth under a flag of truce to ascertain if the French were building a fort at the upper Coos.

Lieutenant of Rogers' Original Company Jan-April 4, 1755 to Nov 1755. Second Lieutenant Rogers' Own March 24, 1756. First Lieutenant July 24, 1756. Captain of Speakman's Feb 24, 1757. Recruiting in winter of 58-9 with Headquarters at Mr. Molville's in Boston in Feb-March. (W.O. 34, 79/0 30.) Retired from Rogers' Rangers Nov 24, 1759.

He was one of the outstanding Major Generals in American Revolution (for an exhaustive record of his services and his life this writer can do no better than to recommend the fine biography by Howard P. Moore).

Died May 8, 1822, 93 years of age.

WILLIAM STARK: 12th Captain

Born April 1, 1724 Londonderry, N.H. First son of Archibald. Elder brother of John. Married in 1754 Mary, sister of Captain William Stinson of Starkstown (Dunbarton). Entered Rogers' Own after Sept 28, 1756 as a Cadet. Second Lieutenant Rogers' Own succeeding John McCurdy (promoted Feb 24, 1757). Captain of a new Company Jan 14, 1758. Served Louisbourg and Quebec campaigns. Discharged with Company Nov 30, 1759 at Boston.

Receiving a War Land Grant in Fryeburg, Maine, he settled there. At outbreak of Revolution he favored the patriot cause, although his son did not. In the winter of 1776 he applied for leave to raise a regiment, but soon after was forced to leave his country for he was caught forging a Massachusetts bill of credit from 16 to 40 shillings and passed it. Retiring within the British lines at New York he was commissioned a Major in the N.H. Volunteers. He is reported to have died May 18, 1781 "while watching a Cricket game on Long Island." His large estate in Freyburg, Maine, valued at 3,345 pounds was confiscated.

SIMON STEVENS: 25th (last) Captain

Of Deerfield, Mass.

Born Sept 3, 1737 at Rutland, Mass. The 3rd son to survive of the famed Capt Phineas Stevens of No. 4, N.H. (who defended the fort with 30 men on April 4, 1747 for 3 days against 400 French and Indians. Younger brother of Lt. Samuel Stevens.

Entered Rogers' Own Company March 20, 1757, as a Cadet. Recommended by Rogers Jan 10, 1758, for a Lieutenancy in J. Stark's. First Lieutenant John Stark's Jan 14, 1758. Captured June 25, 1758, while leading a scout to Northwest Bay, on Lake George. Escaped from Quebec, May 1, 1759, in a canoe down the St. Lawrence River and after a series of odysseys related in Volume II of this *History*, he arrived at Louisbourg in a captured schooner on June 6, 1759. Served in Quebec campaign as an additional Lieutenant in W. Stark's. He was reported wounded at Quebec, July 22, 1759. Stevens wrote a journal of his capture and escape and it was printed and sold by Edes & Gill, in Queen St., Boston, 19 pp 20 cm., in the spring of 1760. On May 3, 1760, he memorialized Amherst from Albany, for a berth in Rogers' Rangers. He received the First Lieutenancy of J. Brewer's, dated March 1, 1760. On July 9, 1760, he was the last officer to receive a Captaincy. He replaced Noah Johnson to the command of his Company. Commission dated "Three Rivers" by Amherst. (W.O. 34, 82/218; 85/2.)

Settled at Number Four, N.H. after the War.

JAMES TUTE: 21st Captain

Born in Hardwick, Mass. Dec 21, 1738, son of James and Kezia. James Tute, Jr. has frequently been misspelled Tate, Fute, Chut, Stoote, Tout, Tuite and even Tutle, which his birth is registered under. Tute's first military service was in the 1756 campaign as a Private in Captain John Catlin's Provincial Company. (His brother Amos was a Ranger under Burke.)

Entered Richard Rogers' Company, Feb 24, 1757, as a Private. Served until Company was disbanded Aug 24, 1757. Remained on at Rogers' Island as a Volunteer in the Corps, until Nov 24, 1757, when he re-enlisted as a Private in Rogers' Own Company. A Sergeant shortly after. Served so conspicuously at the Battle of Rogers' Rock, March 13, 1758, that Rogers recommended him highly and he was commissioned April 7, 1758, First Lieutenant of Shepherd's. Succeeded Shepherd as Captain when he retired from the Corps on July 12, 1759. Captured near La Gallette on Sept 22, 1759, with a detachment of Rangers, while carrying dispatches to Gage from Amherst. Exchanged on Nov 15, 1759. Re-Captured at Crown Point on Lake Champlain, Mar 31, 1760. Exchanged on June 21, 1760, in time to join Captain Rogers' Own in Haviland's advance on Montreal. Discharged with Corps, Nov 11, 1760, at Albany.

Fort No. 4, Charlestown, N.H. Heroically defended by men of the STEVENS family who later became prominent Rogers' Ranger officers. The Fort-a focal point-for St. Francis Raid return. Courtesy Crown Point Road Association.

by R. F. Heinrich. Courtesy National Life Ins. Vt.

Commissioned First Lieutenant in Gorham's Corps of Rangers on the Regular establishment (sometime between 1762-64). Retired on half-pay when Corps was disbanded and petitioned Governor Wentworth with Robert Rogers for a veteran's land grant on June 25, 1764. Tute states his residence as Deerfield, Massachusetts Since Tute (curiously enough) received his Lieutenancy in Gorham's from Wentworth he was entitled to land in N.H. On July 4, 1764, Tute's petition was granted and Wentworth awarded him 2,000 acres.

After his return from England in Jan 1766 Rogers contacted Tute some time after his arrival about the Northwest Passage expedition. Tute joined Rogers at Michilimackinac and on Sept 12, 1766, "Governor Rogers" commissioned him Commander of a "Party for the Discovery of the Northwest Passage from the Atlantic into the Pacific Ocean if any such passage there-be, or for the Discovery of the Great River Ourigan (Oregon) that falls into the Pacific Ocean about the Latitude Fifty." Tute's party consisted of his Secretary, James Stanley Goddard; Jonathan Carver (who he was to pick up near the Falls of St. Anthony), Draughtsman; Joseph Reaume, Interpreter; Andrew Stewart, Commissary; and Augustus Ange, Lorange and Gabriel Loring, Engages. Five days later, on Sept 17 "Captain Tute's" left on their abortive Expedition. They did not return to Michilimackinac until Aug 29, 1767, eleven months later. Goddard was commissioned by Rogers to keep a detailed journal, which he did. A Resume follows:

Left Michilimackinac in a bark canoe Sept 17, at 6 a.m. Saw Chief Mamickquoine at Little Ottawa village on Little Detroit Island on Amanistick River, about 30 leagues from Michilimackinac. Gave Chief a little rum and enticed him to come to Michilimackinac in the spring to see his father (Rogers). Visited Chief Otter of a Menominies village on Manomemacon River; then Fort La Raye, 18 leagues WSW of above River and one mile up River du Renard on N. shore. Next visited Chief Econeme, or the Horse's village of Minomines a half mile up this River. Visited a village of Puentes; the village of Sackin, of Washebones; village of Otagamies; then determined to winter on River du Dard on west side of Mississippi, 12 leagues below Ouaconsang. Built their house when Trader Bruce came down and persuaded Tute to go and winter on a River called Ione. Tute set off Nov 30, on foot with Bruce. A canoe with portion of party's provision preceding them the day before.

Goddard did not meet Tute again until April at La Prairie de La Hun on east side of Mississippi. Tute sent Goddard back to the British post of Fort La Raye for Liquor to induce Indians to visit Rogers at Michilimackinac. Goddard reached the Fort in 11 days and returned in 12, to find that Jonathan Carver had joined Tute. Goddard wrote Rogers before expedition left La Hun, enclosing the different speeches of the Indians with Tute.

Expedition left La Hun on May 21, 1767, in two canoes up the Mississippi. Eighth day arrived at the Chippewa River; decided to skirt Sioux country by proceeding up this river. Visited village on Lake Ottawa, staying six days. Ran out of provisions at end of Lake Superior and sent a canoe off to meet the French canoes from Michilimackinac, which returned the sixth day with a small replenishment. Gave a stand of Colors to Chief of the carrying-place (Chippewa Indians). After consultation found they did not have the necessary provisions to continue and agreed to return to Michilimackinac, arriving Aug 29, 1767.

Shortly after Governor Rogers was confined to await trial for treason and any further Rogers-Tute attempts to discover the Northwest Passage did not materialize. When Rogers was confined at Michilimackinac in December 1767, Tute queried Gage at Montreal on Dec 10, about Rogers' power to send men on the Northwest Passage expedition. Although Gage replied on May 2, 1768, that Rogers had not been given such power, still Tute's expenditures on his Northwest Passage expedition were condoned after Gage probed into the matter. Carver penned a certificate at Michilimackinac on May 26, 1768, to the effect that he had accompanied Tute who was obliged to give large presents to the Indians to win them to the English but that he "used the utmost discretion on that account that was in his power—and by what I have Seen in his accounts that they are very Just as to the publick and perticolar Expences of this voyage."

Tute apparently disposed of his holdings in N.H., for he definitely stayed in the west as a trader. During the winter of 1771-1772 he was residing among the Indians in the Illinois country. He was reported to have cut off an Indian's nose on the way back in the spring "but not without good reason." (Apparently Tute had taken a squaw and suspected her of infidelity—for the cutting off of an Indian woman's nose was one of the punishments for such an offense.)

Tute soon plied his trade south-westward toward Fort Dauphin. His career as a fur-trader ended abruptly on the western plain when he succumbed to the smallpox epidemic of 1781-82. There is no mention of Tute ever marrying.

Sources: For much of this sketch (other than Tute's service in Rogers' Rangers) this writer is indebted to Robert C. Davis of the University of Wisconsin, who is writing an exhaustive Life of Jonathan Carver.

(Sheldon, G: *History of Deerfield, Massachusetts,* 2: 348-9. L.C. Kellogg: *History of Bernardston, Massachusetts,* 512. *Vital Record of Hardwick,* 518. *N.H. Provincial Papers,* VII: 1, and *N.H. State Papers,* XXVI: 127-29, 652. Louise Kellogg, *British Regime in Wisconsin and the Northwest,* 55-6. J. Carver: "Travels." *Can. Hist. Rev.,* XIII, 1932, 387-402. *Correspondence of Gage,* p 56n. K. Roberts: *Northwest Passage,* Vol. II. *Goddard's Journal:* in McGill Univ. J. Mayer *Major Robert Rogers, Trader,* 396-7.)

SOLOMON UHHAUNWAUMUT: 24th Captain

A Stockbridge Mohegan Indian Warrior from Stockbridge, Mass.

Private in Jacob Cheeksaunkun's May 27-Sept 1, 1756. Ensign Sept 2-Nov 11, 1756.

Lieutenant of Jacob Naunauphtaunk's Feb 6, 1758. Captained the remnants of the two Jacobs' Companies after their capture in 1759 to their disbandment at end of campaign.

Captain in 1760, of the Stockbridge Mohegan Company raised then. Commissioned May 30, 1760. Discharged with Company Nov 11, 1760.

Solomon was a principal chief of the Stockbridges by the time of the Revolution. On Sept 1, 1775, he pledged the Allegiance of the Stockbridges to the Americans.

JOSEPH WAIT: 20th Captain. (Sometimes spelled "Waite.")

Born in Massachusetts. Later lived in Alstead, N.H.

Saw border scouting service in Captain Eleazer Melvin's Provincial Company in 1754. In 1757, he was on the Lake George front as a Corporal in John Burks' Company of Provincial Rangers. He served with such distinction that he was called to the attention of Rogers who recommended him for a Lieutenancy in Burbank's proposed Company on Jan 10, 1758. Commissioned by Loudoun Jan 14, 1758, Ensign in Rogers' Own Company. Served heroically at Rogers' Rock. Promoted April 7, 1758, to fill Burbank's First Lieutenancy vacancy in Rogers' Own. Succeeded Wendell as Captain on May 11, 1759. Served in St. Francis Raid. Accompanied Rogers to Detroit in 1760. Served with Company in West Indies 1761-2. Discharged with Company about June 16, 1762.

Settled on a veteran's land grant in N.H.

At outbreak of Revolution Wait was a Captain in Allen's Regiment and present at the capture of Ticonderoga in 1775, although this fact is disputed by some authorities.

He was a member from Claremont of the N.H. Provincial Congress. Became Lieutenant-Colonel of Timothy Bedel's N.H. Militia Regiment raised to help cover the retreat of Montgomery's Army from Canada. (This Regiment was marched into Canada and at a Fort called "The Cedars" was disgracefully surrendered by the Adjutant, as Bedel and Wait were both absent at the time.) Three months later Wait was mortally wounded in a severe skirmish before the Battle of Valcour Island. He died a few days later on Sept 28, 1776. He was buried in Clarendon, Vt., where a monument marks his grave. (*New England Quarterly,* III, 19-30. Society of Colonial

Wars, *Index of Ancestors*, 502. Potter, *Military History of New Hampshire*, I, pp 286-7.)

HENRY ISAAC WENDELL: 25th Captain
Born in the Mohawk Valley near Schoharie.
A trusted friend of the Oneidas.
Ensign in Pepperell's 51st Regiment. Stationed at Fort Williams (Oneida Carrying Place, later Fort Stanwix) in 1756. He was frequently employed as a diplomatic agent with his friends the Oneidas. When he was slated to be transferred to Oswego, the whole Oneida Nation protested so vigorously that he was kept at the Oneida Carrying Place for a time, and avoided capture when Oswego fell. During the winter of 56-57 he was ordered to Boston to recruit for the 51st. Ordered to New York by Loudoun he memorialized him on April 8, 1757, asking for duty in Albany (to be near his family, who were sick there) over the batteau-men transporting provisions up to the Mohawk River forts; being well acquainted with the service and terrain. He also asks for his "Slap Gold" and baggage money, as he had to pay for its conveyance from Boston to N.Y.—and spent all of his pay in recruiting through the winter of 56-7. Irked at Loudoun's delay in providing for him, Wendell penned him again ten days later, on April 18, stating that due to his infirmity he was incapable of future duty and resigned any claims for half-pay (his 51st Regiment being disbanded), pension, or any other reward for past services. Loudoun, however, sent Wendell up to Sir William Johnson at Johnson's Hall, who recommended him for an agent's commission with the Oneidas. But manifold jealous aspersions against Wendell kept him from obtaining his commission. As late as Jan 1758, he was petitioning Abercromby for the post, or, for a Company of Rangers. Abercromby recommended him to Loudoun on Jan 8, 1758, and Loudoun reshuffled Rogers' recommendations for McCurdy's new Ranger Company—and commissioned Wendell First Lieutenant of the Company on Jan 14, 1758. However, on March 25, 1758 he was promoted to Captain the Company he proposed for Fort Stanwix service.

After repeated mutinous behaviour and frequent desertions by his men he asked to be relieved of his command and willingly gave up the Captaincy to Joseph Wait on May 11, 1759. In the spring of 1760, Wendell was petitioning Amherst asking to be returned to duty. He also relates how one of his deserters, George Wendecker, had accosted him at his home in Albany demanding payment for the time he had deserted (18 months). Wendell threw him out of doors and told him to join Wait's and serve his time out. But the audacious Wendecker, immediately obtained a lawful writ of 500 pounds against Wendell and recommended other Ranger deserters to do the same. Wendell requested Amherst to look into this matter. Though Amherst was amazed at Wendecker's gall he recommended Wendell seek legal aid. (LO 1101, 3319, 1098, 1104, 3374-A, 3727, 5360. AB 314, 923-1&2. W.O. 34 79/114.)

THE FIRST LIEUTENANTS

JOSIAH BANCK (BANK): 19th First Lieutenant
First Lieutenant in Ogden's in March 1760. Served in West
Indies with Company 1761-2. Discharged about June 16, 1762,
at N.Y.

JOHN BUTLER: 20th First Lieutenant
Of Boston, Mass. (Also Framingham?)
Entered McCurdy's as Ensign after April, 1758. Second
Lieutenant by April 7, 1759. First Lieutenant by April 29, 1760.
Received capitulations of Forts Miamis and Quiatenon and
garrisoned Miamis through winter of 1760-1 to Oct 1761.
Discharged with his platoon at N.Y., Jan 24, 1762.
Later, in Revolutionary War, commanded "Butler's Rangers"
(Loyalists).

EDWARD CROFTON: 12th First Lieutenant
Of England.
An English Volunteer who had served as a Volunteer in his
friend, Sir John Whiteford's Regiment in England. Hoping for
quicker advancement he arrived in North America in 1757 as a
free-lance volunteer, not attached to any Corps. He involved
himself in a serious quarrel with Major Darby and petitioned
Loudoun to allow him to engage in a duel with him. (LO 5992;
4816.) Instead, Loudoun attached Crofton to Rogers' Rangers
as a Volunteer when the Cadet Company was formed. Rogers
liked his fearless personality and quick adaptability to Ranging
methods and he recommended him to Loudoun on Jan 10,
1758, for a Lieutenancy in his own company. Upon being
notified of his appointment, Crofton wrote Loudoun politely
refusing because it would not give him rank and asked that he
might be placed in some Regiment as a Volunteer, or be
allowed to return to England and Whiteford's Regiment.

Crofton was evidently prevailed upon to accept the commission for Loudoun commissioned him Second Lieutenant of John Stark's Jan 14, 1758. He served with distinction at Rogers' Rock, March 13, 1758, commanding Rogers' left flank. He was one of the two officers to return with Rogers. He carried Rogers' official journal of the action to General Howe. Anxious to serve against Louisbourg he was given the Second Lieutenancy in J. Brewer's Company left vacant by the death of Archibald Campbell at Rogers' Rock. His transfer was dated March 30, 1758. Accompanying the Company to Louisbourg he served with distinction and was promoted to the First Lieutenancy during the winter of 1758-9. In the Quebec campaign, Wolfe realizing Crofton's latent abilities chose him to perform a difficult assignment prior to the Battle of the Plains, its nature not clearly discernible. (Wolfe to Monckton from Montmorency, Aug 04, 1759, in Northcliffe Coll., Vol XXII, p 149.) Wolfe awarded Crofton with a commission in the 45th as Second Lieutenant, post-dating it Sept 25, 1759. He served in that capacity until Feb 1761, when he was killed at Boston in a duel with a fellow officer over a question of rank. His commanding officer, Lieut-Colonel Montagu Wilmot of the 45th, clearly indicates his own sympathy when he reported the affair to General Amherst on Feb 8, 1761: "I have the honour to acquaint your Excellency with an unfortunate accident that happen'd in the 45th Regt...Lieutenant Crofton (who had been put into the Regiment by General Wolf over all the Ensigns from being an officer of Rangers) having as I am informed treated Lieutenant Burns with very opprobrious Language in Public, laid that unhappy Gentleman under a sort of fatal necessity of acting in opposition to his Duty by seeking a revenge in a manner contrary to the articles of War, the result of which was, that Lieutenant Crofton received a Pistol shot, of which he died the Day after." (W.O. 34, 84-87, 177.)

ROBERT D'ARCY: 15th First Lieutenant
     Of New York City.
     Entered Rogers' Rangers July 12, 1759, replacing James Tute as First Lieutenant of Shepherd's (Tute's). He was a mapmaker and draughtsman of unusual merit and soon established himself high in Amherst's esteem when he made him a map of South Bay and adjacent country when Amherst was endeavoring to learn more about that terrain in Aug-Sept 1759. On leave with half-pay during 1759-60 winter. Second Lieutenant of J. Brewer's in March 1760. First Lieutenant July 9, 1760. Discharged with Company on Nov 11, 1760.
     Ensign in 95th Regiment April 22, 1762.
     By 1772, he was stationed in the Drawing Room of the Tower of London where he was busily engaged in drawing maps. In June 1773, he was one of twelve British officers of high standing to recommend the granting of Rogers' petition to the King to discover the Northwest Passage. He signed his name on the petition as "Captain D'Arcy, aid-de-camp to General Amherst." In Carver's petition to the Lord Commissioners on May 18, 1772, to allow Rogers to lead an expedition to search for a Northwest Passage he recommends D'Arcy to accompany the expedition. His name was frequently misspelled Dorsey, Darcey and Darcy.

JAMES FAULKNER: 8th First Lieutenant
     Of Charlestown (No. 4), N.H.
     First Lieutenant Neale's new Company April 7, 1758. Resigned in winter of 58-59.

JOHN FLETCHER: 13th First Lieutenant
     Of Chesterfield, N.H.
     Lieutenant of M. Brewer's April 1, 1759. First Lieutenant of D. Brewer's May 24, 1760. Captured near La Prairie Aug 27, 1759. Exchanged Nov 15, 1759. Discharged with Company on Nov 11, 1760.

WILLIAM HAIR: 7th First Lieutenant
First Lieutenant of Wendell's new Company March 25, 1758. Evidently resigned about May 11, 1759.

ROBERT HOLMES: 11th First Lieutenant
Son of a Livery-Keeper in N.H.
Private of Rogers' Own, July 23, 1756.
Second Lieutenant of Neale's new Company April 7, 1758. First Lieutenant by winter of 58-9 when Johnson replaced Neale. Accompanied Rogers to Detroit in 1760. Escorted the French garrison from Detroit to Pittsburgh and Amherst at N.Y., where he arrived on Feb 4, 1761. Amherst rewarded him with an Ensigncy in the 60th, dated Dec 12, 1760 which he purchased for 100 pounds, borrowing the amount from Rogers. After Holmes' death, Rogers was dunning the Regimental paymaster on Aug 12, 1763 for payment.
Much to his chagrin, Holmes' first assignment was the isolated command of Fort Miamis on the River Maumee (relieving Ranger Lieut. John Butler). In 1763, when Detroit was attacked, Holmes learned of it from a French trader and was on his guard. However, on May 27, 1763, a young Indian girl who lived with him, came to tell him that a squaw lay dangerously ill in a wigwam near the fort, and urged him to go to her relief. Holmes, having complete confidence in the girl, waived his customary caution and followed her out of the fort to be led into an ambush and killed. His garrison, now without a leader, soon surrendered. (W.O. 34, 85/245. Boquet Coll: A16-p 90; A17-p 76; A19-2-p 362.)

SAMUEL KENNEDY: 1st First Lieutenant
Lieutenant in Winslow's expedition to build Fort Halifax on Kennebec River in 1754.
First Lieutenant Speakman's Sept 1, 1756.
Killed Jan 21, 1757 at La Barbue Creek.

THOMAS LAWRENCE: 5th First Lieutenant

Of N.H.

Recommended by Rogers on Jan 10, 1758 for an eleventh Company Captaincy. When rejected by Loudoun, Rogers recommended him for the First Lieutenancy of J. Brewer's new Company on Jan 14, 1758. Commissioned by Loudoun Jan 14, 1758, First Lieutenant of J. Brewer's. Probably served until disbandment of Company at Boston, Nov 30, 1759.

JOHN McDUFFE (DUFFY): 4th First Lieutenant

Of Londonderry, N.H. Born Sept 14, 1723, second son of Daniel and Ruth.

Recommended by Rogers Jan 10, 1758 for the Captaincy of a proposed 10th Company.

Commissioned Jan 14, 1758, First Lieutenant of W. Stark's new Company. Discharged with disbanded Company at Boston Nov 30, 1759.

ANDREW McMULLEN: 10th First Lieutenant

Of Worcester, Mass. He came to America from Ireland about 1754.

Entered Rogers' Rangers Feb 25, 1757, as a Private in Rogers' Own. Commissioned by Abercrombie, June 26, 1758, Second Lieutenant of Burbank's. First Lieutenant after Mark Noble's retirement at close of campaign.

First Lieutenant of J. Rogers' in 1760.

Discharged Nov 11, 1760, with Company.

Married Hannah Osgood, of Rumford, daughter of James Osgood, Nov 12, 1761. "The same year he commenced trade in the store that now stands on the N.E. corner of Main and Pleasant Sts. (Concord, N.H.), which was then a small one-story shop, standing as it now does, partly in the street. Here he continued to trade for several years; one year in partnership with Timothy Walker Jr., and afterwards with John Stevens, who added a second story to it. In 1767 or 68, he and General Stark received each a grant of land from Governor Wentworth of N.H. for war services. The grant was located in Conway and vicinity. In August 1774, he removed to Conway, to take possession. Two of his wife's brothers, James and Benjamin Osgood of Concord, had preceded him. Here, in the cultivation of one of the most valuable farms on Saco River[1] (where his only remaining son, Gilbert, now resides), he passed the remainder of his life—repeatedly representing the town in the State Legislature, and faithfully discharging his duty as a citizen and a magistrate."

"He became the leading man in the community maintaining sort of baronial estate with colored servants. He was also the first of the long line of tavern-keepers in the township." (*N.H. American Guide Series*, pp. 281-2). A photo of his house/inn in Conway may be seen on p 44 of *Town of Conway, N.H. Bicentennial*, 1763-1963. Crosby Milliman swore the original patent deed to McMullen's famous house.

McMullen was Colonel of the 11th N.H. Militia Regiment until Aug, 1774, when he moved to Conway. He died Nov 6, 1800, aged 70 years. His wife died in 1827, aged 84. (Bouton, *History of Concord.* Society of Colonial Wars, *Index*, p 324.)

MARK NOBLE: 9th First Lieutenant
Of Dunbarton, N.H.
First Lieutenant of Burbank's April 7, 1758 (replacing J. Pottinger killed at Rogers' Rock). Probably resigned at end of campaign.

JOHN PATTEN: 14th First Lieutenant
Entered Rogers' Rangers Mar 30, 1758, as Second Lieutenant of McCurdy's new Company when Hazen refused to accept. First Lieutenant April 6, 1759, when Hazen was promoted to the Captaincy. Served with such distinction at the Battle of Ste. Foy that he was rewarded the following day (April 29, 1760) with an Ensign's commission in the 48th Regiment at Quebec. Lieutenant in 48th April 26, 1762.

---

[1] The whole intervale on the east side of the Saco River

NOAH PORTER: 2nd First Lieutenant
   Of Connecticut.
   Entered Corps May 25, 1757 as a Private in Rogers' Own. One of the chief instigators of the Rangers' 1757 "Whipping Post Mutiny." Confined at Fort Edward until Rogers obtained his release in Jan 1758, when he was discharged. However, Rogers recommended him to Loudoun Jan 10, 1758 for the First Lieutenancy of M. Brewer's new Company.
   Commissioned same Jan 14, 1758. Resigned with M. Brewer at end of 1758. Re-enlisted as Private into Rogers' Own on Aug 11, 1760.

JAMES POTTINGER: 3rd First Lieutenant
   From England.
   Served with King George in Flanders as a Volunteer. After the Battle of Val he obtained His Majesty's permission to go to Bergenopzoom, in which Siege he served until it was taken by the French, after which King George commissioned him an Ensign in the 44th. In 1752 Pottinger purchased a Lieutenancy in the Regiment. Served in Europe until start of French and Indian War when his Corps came across to serve in Braddock's fateful expedition. After Braddock's Defeat in 1755, Pottinger's career started downwards. His indiscretions with a camp-follower led him to become an alcoholic and loaded besides with debt contracted to purchase his Lieutenancy, he was obliged to leave the service. Loudoun, in response to Pottinger's plea for an opportunity to regain "the character he once had in the army," placed him under Rogers' wing as a Rogers' Ranger Cadet on Sept 14, 1757.
   Rogers recommended him for the First Lieutenancy of Bulkeley's on Jan 11, 1758.
   Commissioned same by Loudoun Jan 14, 1758.
   Killed March 13, 1758, at Rogers' Rock, leaving an orphaned daughter by his former mistress.

JOSEPH SENTER: 6th First Lieutenant
Of Londonderry, N.H. Born March 1724, second son of
Benjamin and Abigail.
Recommended by Rogers Jan 10, 1758, for the First
Lieutenancy of J. Rogers' new Company. Commissioned same
by Loudoun Jan 14, 1758. Discharged with Company at Boston
on Nov 30, 1759.
Colonel of a N.H. Militia Regiment raised in 1777 to
defend Rhode Island in the American Revolution.

ARCHIBALD STARK: 21st First Lieutenant
Born in Londonderry in 1730, second son of Archibald, Sr.
Brother of John Stark.
Entered Rogers' Own on Oct 5, 1756. Sergeant in J. Stark's,
Feb 24, 1757. Recommended by Rogers Jan 10, 1758, for an
Ensigncy. Ensign April 7 or 28, 1758, commissioned by
Abercrombie, Second Lieutenant in Johnson's by spring of
1759. First Lieutenant in Stevens' July 9, 1760. Discharged with
Company Nov 11, 1760.
Died at Hopkinton, N.H., in 1819.

DAVID STONE: 22nd First Lieutenant
Of Petersham, Mass.
Second Lieutenant in Shepherd's (Tute's) by spring of 1759.
Second Lieutenant in J. Rogers' in 1760. First Lieutenant in
Wait's by spring of 1761. Served with Company in West Indies
1761-2. Discharged with Company about June 16, 1762.

NATHAN STONE: 17th First Lieutenant
Served in Nova Scotia 1755-57.
Second Lieutenant Rogers' Own April 7, 1758 replacing
Increase Moore killed at Rogers' Rock.
Captured with Lieut. Stevens June 25, 1758 near Northwest
Bay, Lake George. Taken prisoner to Ticonderoga same day.
Following day taken to an Indian village. Sold to the French
and kept a prisoner at Quebec on parole in a private house.

Roomed with Lieut. Stevens and Major Israel Putnam. Allowed 5 pence, 1 farthing sterling per day subsistence money. Planned to escape with Stevens but held up by winter of 1758-9. Refused to attempt to escape in the spring with Stevens by water. Exchanged Nov 15, 1759. Detached to No. 4, N.H., on that date, with 25 Rangers to act as scouts for winter. Discharged with Corps on Nov 11, 1760.

Petitioned Amherst from Albany, July 1, 1761, asking for relief: "...Had the misfortune in 1760 of being badly wounded (in Bougainville's Retreat in Sept—wounded in the foot) whereof he hath as yet not recovered and hath but little hopes at present to expect that he ever shall..." and remained at great expense, his pay cut off since last Oct 24th. On April 12, 1762, Ensign Alexander Miln of a S.C. Independent Company was court-martialed and dismissed. Stone succeeded him. Amherst wrote Grant on April 30, 1762, "This Gentleman was much wounded at Isle au Noix, but being now recovered and well recommended to me I have thought proper to provide for him in this vacancy..." (W.O. 34, 92/87; 92/106; 87/1.)

STUBENS (STEVENS): 16th First Lieutenant
First Lieutenant in Wendell's by May 11, 1759.

RICHARD VAN TYNE: 18th First Lieutenant
Entered Ogden's new Company in March 1760 as First Lieutenant. Commanded winter (1760-61) Postal Service platoon of Rangers between Crown Point and Montreal with his headquarters at Isle aux Noix. Served in Ogden's in West Indies 1761-2. Killed Jan 24, 1762, at Battle of Morne Tortenson on Martinique.

THE SECOND LIEUTENANTS

NATHANIEL ABBOTT: 1st Second Lieutenant
Born in Andover, Mass., in 1696. When about 30 years old he moved to Penacook, N.H. with its first settlers. During King George's War he served in various scouting Companies guarding the frontiers of N.H.
June 25-Oct 2, 1748, he served in Captain John Goffe's Company as a Private.
From April 24-Oct 24, 1755, he was Lieutenant of the 5th Company of Blanchard's N.H. Regiment.
Entered Rogers' Rangers in Aug, 1756, as the Second Lieutenant of Richard Rogers' new Ranger Company. He was not commissioned by Loudoun until Feb 25, 1757. Served in Company until its capture at Fort William Henry Aug 9, 1757, when it was disbanded following the terms of capitulation.
Died in 1770, aged 74 years.

PHINEAS ATHERTON (ETHERINGTON):
26th Second Lieutenant
Born in Lancaster, Mass., Feb 17, 1740, son of Amos and his wife Elizabeth Harris.
Owned a house and 100 acres of cultivated land. In 1755 he was a volunteer in the expedition against the Acadians in Nova Scotia. In 1757, he was on the Lake George front in Capt. Thomas Hartwell's Company in Frye's Provincial Regiment.
A Private in Wendell's new Ranger Company March 30, 1758. Ensign by early 1759. Second Lieutenant by end of 1759. Recommended by Rogers on May 4, 1760, for the Lieutenancy of a proposed new Company under McMullen.
Served in Rogers' 1760 Detroit expedition. Discharged March 24, 1761.
Served as a Loyalist in the Revolution. Appointed in Jan, 1777, Lieutenant in the King's Royal Regiment of N.Y. The following July was Provost-Marshal to Burgoyne's army and he

was taken prisoner with this army in Oct, 1777, and kept prisoner until Nov, 1782, "labouring under every inconvenience that his incensed neighbours could devise."

On Jan 26, 1784, Colonel Abijah Willar vouched for his integrity as a firm Loyalist. In 1788 he was imprisoned for debt in the Marshalsea Prison in London, where, according to his petition, he had lain for over two months in great distress and destitute even of the common necessities of life. On Nov 24, of the same year he wrote a letter regarding his property. On July 26, 1784, he gave evidence in support of his claim and his application for a pension. He was apparently in England at the outbreak of the American Revolution and returned home immediately. His claim of 140 pounds for the loss of his property was met with a reward of 110 pounds. Atherton was a signatory to the memorial of Jonathan Carver, Moses Park and Isaac DaCosta dated May 18, 1772, praying to be appointed members of a proposed expedition under Rogers to discover a Northwest Passage. (E.A. Jones, *Loyalists of Massachusetts*, pp 10-11. H. S. Nourse, *Military Annals of Lancaster, Massachusetts*, pp 42, 59-60. A petition is printed in H. E. Edgerton's *The Royal Commission on the Losses and Services of American Loyalists*, pp 90-1. *Sir William Johnson Papers*, VIII, p 134. I am particularly indebted to Robert C. Davis of the University of Wisconsin for clues on Atherton.)

ARCHIBALD CAMPBELL, SR.: 8th Second Lieutenant

A Scotch Volunteer from the 42nd Highlanders. Brother of Captain-Lieutenant John Campbell of the same Regiment. Archibald had served as a soldier of fortune in the Dutch Army for four years. Petitioned Loudoun, Nov 23, 1757, for a commission. (LO 4888.) Pushed by Loudoun for a Lieutenancy in Rogers' Rangers which he gave him on Jan 14, 1758, in J. Brewer's new Company. Killed March 13, 1758, at Rogers' Rock.

GEORGE CAMPBELL: 21st Second Lieutenant
Entered Corps in spring of 1759 as Second Lieutenant of Burbank's. Unprovided for in 1760 Ranger Companies and discharged May 7, 1760. Entered Regular Army in spring of 1760, with Ensigncy in the 42nd dated May 8, 1759; Lieutenant, same Corps, July 24, 1762.

ABERNATHAN (ABERNETHY) CARGILL (GARGYLL): 23rd Second Lieutenant
Originally of Newcastle, Maine, son of David and Mary (Abernethy) Cargill of Newcastle. Residing in Boston when he enlisted as a Private in J. Stark's on Dec 25, 1757.
Promoted to the Second Lieutenancy of Shepherd's about July 12, 1759. Rogers notes on May 4, 1760, that Cargill is "on command at Albany." Recommended by Colonel John Darby of the 17th Regiment to Amherst on July 26, 1760, for an Ensigncy vacancy in his Regiment. Commissioned same, Sept 18, 1760. (W.O. 34, 51/75.)

JAMES CLARKE (CLARK): 14th Second Lieutenant
Of the Merrimack Valley, N.H.
Entered Rogers' original Company in Jan, 1755, as a Private. Promoted to Sergeant after Nov 24, 1757. For gallantry at Rogers' Rock, he was promoted to the Second Lieutenancy of J. Stark's on April 7, 1758. Probably retired from Corps at close of 1758.

FRANCIS CREED: 13th Second Lieutenant
English Vol. from 27th. Nephew to Lord Blakney. Petitioned Loudoun Jan 1, 1758 for commission (LO 6325). Ranger Cadet Sept 14, 1757. Distinguished himself at Rogers' Rock. Commissioned by Abercrombie after Battle. Second Lieutenant in Shepherd's on April 6, 1758 (replacing S. Gilman, resigned). Left the Corps for the Regulars to replace Ensign Balfour of the 27th. (AB 96.) His Ensigncy was dated March 27, 1758. Promoted to a Lieutenancy in the 34th, July 27, 1762.

THOMAS (WILLIAM) CUNNINGHAM:
4th Second Lieutenant
Private of Rogers' Own, Nov 25, 1755 to Feb 24, 1757. Recommended by Rogers on Dec 31, 1756, for a Ranger Officer's berth. Ensign, Rogers' Own, Feb 24, 1757 (replaced W. Stark, promoted). Second Lieutenant Bulkeley's, April 25, 1757. Taken with Smallpox at Halifax, he retired July 16, 1757.

PETER DEGART: 12th Second Lieutenant
Second Lieutenant of Wendell's new Company, March 26, 1758. Evidently retired from the Company at end of campaign.

JOSEPH DUQUIPE: 27th Second Lieutenant
A Mohegan Indian Warrior from Connecticut
Recommended by Rogers for the Ensigncy of Moses Brewer's new Company on Jan 10-11, 1758. Commissioned same Jan 14, 1758. Resigned end of campaign. Re-entered Corps in May, 1760, as Lieutenant of Solomon's. Commanded a platoon of Mohegan Rangers in Rogers' Detroit Expedition, who served as the picket of the detachment.

JACOB FARRINGTON: 26th Second Lieutenant
Of Andover, Mass. Born March 16, 1734-5. Son of Daniel.
Ensign of Neale's new Company April 7, 1758. Second Lt Johnson's Co in 1759. Promoted to First Lieutenant on July 9, 1760, when Simon Stevens was promoted to command the Company after Johnson's death.
Served conspicuously in the St. Francis Raid and at the Battle of Pointe au Fer.
Commanded the platoon of Rogers' Rangers in the Cherokee-English War, 1761, to Aug 26th when he entered Rogers' S.C. Independent Company of Regulars as a Volunteer. His anticipation of a commission did not develop, for no vacancy occurred.

BENJAMIN FOSSIT: 10th Second Lieutenant
Recommended by Rogers on Jan 10, 1758 for the Ensigncy of J. Rogers' new Company.
Commissioned Jan 17, 1758, Second Lieutenant of J. Rogers'. Died in March 1759. (W.O. 34, 54/122.)

SAMUEL GILMAN: 2nd Second Lieutenant
Of Exeter, N.H.
Served as Ensign of 2nd Company of Meserve's N.H. Regiment in 1756.
Second Lieutenant of Shepherd's new Ranger Company, Feb 29, 1757. Resigned April 6, 1758.
Captain of 7th Company, 2nd N.H. Regiment in American Revolution.

WILLIAM HOLDEN: 25th Second Lieutenant
Of N.H.
Recommended by Rogers on Jan 10, 1758 for the 1st Lieutenancy of a proposed new Company of Rangers under Thomas Lawrence. But this 11th Company was not raised. Ensign in J. Rogers', Sept 26, 1759. Second Lieutenant J. Brewer's, Sept 26, 1759. Discharged with Company at Boston, Nov 30, 1759.

STEPHEN HOLLAND: 19th Second Lieutenant
Of Rumford, N.H. Born about 1736.
Sergeant in Richard Rogers' July 24, 1756.
Ensign, Feb 25, 1757, replacing Caleb Page killed. Discharged with Company at Capitulation of Fort William Henry, Aug 9, 1757. Re-entered Corps June 8, 1758, as Ensign of J. Rogers' Company. Second Lieutenant of Company April 1, 1759, succeeding B. Fossit—died.
Left Rogers' Rangers Sept 25, 1759, to enter Dank's Rangers as Lieutenant. Purchased his First Lieutenancy in Gorham's battalion of Regular Rangers on Sept 25, 1761, for 275 pounds sterling (highly recommended by Gorham). (W.O. 34, 12/74-6;

92/167-9.) Left Gorham's Rangers about May 14, 1762, selling his Lieutenancy to "Mr. How."

Ensign in 52nd, dated April 22, 1762. Lieutenant, 52nd, Aug 30, 1771? A half-pay officer residing in Londonderry, N.H. by time of American Revolution. Served with Americans at Siege of Boston as Lieutenant-Colonel of a N.H. Regiment. Afterwards went to N.Y. and joined the British. Commissioned Major in the Prince of Wales American Volunteers. After the peace he received a grant of land in Ireland as remuneration for his confiscated estate in North America valued at 10,000 pounds. (Moore's *Stark*, 113.)

JOSEPH JOHNSON: 11th Second Lieutenant

A Mohegan Indian Warrior.

Recommended by Rogers for the Second Lieutenancy of M. Brewer's new Company on Jan 10, 1758. Commissioned same, Jan 14, 1758.

Resigned at end of year.

JOSHUA LOCK: 20th Second Lieutenant

Of Worcester, Mass.

Second Lieutenant of M. Brewer's, May 11, 1759. Stationed at Stillwater for campaign. Ordered to Crown Point with his platoon on Nov 2, 1759. (W.O. 34, 79/112; 81/113.) Second Lieutenant of D. Brewer's new Company May 24, 1760, but did not re-enter Corps in '60.

CAESAR McCORMICK: 15th Second Lieutenant

Entered Corps as a Volunteer in Rogers' Own, sometime from July 24-Nov 24, 1757.

Recommended for Ensigncy in Rogers' Own by Rogers on Jan 11, 1758. Commissioned Ensign of McCurdy's, Jan 14, 1758. Second Lieutenant of W. Stark's about Oct 15, 1758.

Captured Nov 15, 1758, at head of Peticodiac River, N.B. Exchanged in time to take an active part in the Siege of Quebec. Attached to D. Brewer's in June, when J. Lock did not re-enter the service in 1760. His pay started from Feb 20, 1760 (the date he started recruiting). Served as Adjutant in Rogers' Detroit Expedition in 1760. (W.O. 34, 49/167.) A trader at Detroit at time of 1763 Siege in Pontiac's War. Joined Rogers' Ranger Company when it arrived.

INCREASE MOORE: 6th Second Lieutenant
  Sergeant in Speakman's, Aug 1, 1756.
  Served at La Barbue Creek and wounded slightly in arm.
  Ensign in J. Stark's, Feb 26, 1757.
  Succeeded Walter as a supernumerary Second Lieutenant in Rogers' Own—between Aug-Nov, 1757.
  Killed March 13, 1758, at Rogers' Rock.

WILLIAM MOORE (MORRIS): 7th Second Lieutenant
  Of Stratham, N.H.
  Private in Rogers' Own, June 1, 1756.
  Sergeant, July 23, 1756 to Sept 28, 1756, when demoted to Private.
  Captured Jan 21, 1757, at La Barbue Creek. Remained one month at Ticonderoga, then taken to Montreal. Escaped May 7, 1757. Arriving at Fort William Henry, May 18, 'much fatigued.' Arrived New York May 31, where he was granted an audience with Loudoun, who gave him a Sergeant's berth in the 22nd. However he re-entered Rogers' Own, May 31, as a Volunteer.
  Ensign, Aug 8, 1757, in Bulkeley's.
  On sick list, Nov 24, 1757 roll.
  Recommended by Rogers on Jan 10-11, 1758, for the Second Lieutenancy of Rogers' Own. Commissioned same, Jan 14, 1758. Captured in 1759. Two years prisoner. He sent a journal with his petition for captivity pay but not found. (Coleman, p. 370.)

NATHANIEL OGDEN: 16th Second Lieutenant
  Brother of Captain Jonathan Ogden of N.Y. Provincial Ranging Company.
  Lieutenant in Wendell's in late 1758.

Recommended by Gage for the Captaincy of Wendell's. When not given the Captaincy, he resigned. In March 1760, he entered Ogden's as the Ensign. Commanded the Rangers' advance post at Siege of Fort Levis, Aug 5, 1760. (W.O. 34, 82/302.) Served with Company in West Indies, being promoted to Lieutenant. Discharged with Company at N.Y. about June 16, 1762.

WILLIAM HENDRICK PHILLIPS: 5th Second Lieutenant
Resided near Albany. Born about 1719. Of Dutch-French-Indian origin.
Entered Rogers' Own as Private on June 1, 1756. Sergeant after Oct 24, 1756. Recommend by Rogers for an officer's berth on Dec 11, 1756. For distinguished service at La Barbue Creek, Jan 21, 1757, he was promoted to the Ensigncy of Hobbs' (Bulkeley's) on Feb 27, 1757. Second Lieutenant Bulkeley's, Aug 8, 1757 (replacing T. Cunningham, retired). Recommended by Rogers on Jan 10, 1758, for First Lieutenancy of Bulkeley's.
Captured March 13, 1758, at Rogers' Rock.
Escaped same year. Due to Abercrombie's contract with Rogers, Phillips' Lieutenancy had been filled and he served the 1759 campaign and winter of 59-60 as a Volunteer in Rogers' Own. Recommended by Rogers May 4, 1760, for Ensigncy of Wait's. Received the Ensigncy of J. Brewer's on May 24, 1760. Discharged with Company Nov 11th.
After the war Phillips lived for some time in Rumford (Concord), where he married Miss Eleanor Eastman, daughter of Ebenezer, Jr., by whom he had a son. About 1784, his wife joined the Shakers at Canterbury, N.H. but Phillips said he "could not dance, and would not join." Eleanor resumed her maiden name—leaving Phillips. She died of consumption, Nov 17, 1816, aged 70 years. After his wife left him, Phillips led a roving unsettled life—fishing, hunting and stealing; sometimes working as a blacksmith, at which he was experienced and at times worked as a laborer. He lived a while with his wife's brother, Stilson Eastman, a fellow Ranger. At length he became a pauper and according to the times was "bid off" to be

supported at the town charge. He lived several years in the family of Richard Potter of Anthony Potter, of Joseph Potter and Ebenezer Tenney on the Loudoun road. When he died in 1819 age 100, he was residing in Northfield, N.H. (Bouton: *History of Concord.*)

THOMAS REED: 24th Second Lieutenant
Sergeant, J. Stark's Feb 24, 1757.
Recommended by Rogers for Ensigncy of J. Brewer's new Company on Jan 11, 1758. Commissioned Ensign in W. Stark's March 30, 1758 (replacing Andrew Ross killed March 13, at Rogers' Rock). Promoted to Second Lieutenant Sept 25, 1759 in J. Rogers'. Discharged at Boston on Nov 30, 1759 with Company.

CHARLES ROGERS: 9th Second Lieutenant
Of New Hampshire.
Recommended by Rogers Jan 10, 1758 for the First Lieutenancy of a proposed 10th Company to be Captained by John McDuffy. Recommended the next day for Second Lieutenancy W. Stark's. Commissioned same—Jan 14, 1758. On Oct 15, 1758, he desired leave to resign his commission on account of his health (petition granted by Monckton).

SAMUEL STEVENS: 17th Second Lieutenant
Of New Hampshire.
Entered J. Stark's Feb 25, 1758 as Private. Promoted to Lieutenant of Burbank's after April 24, 1758.
Failed in his assignment to wait with supplies at Wells River for Rogers' St. Francis Indian Raiders in 1759. At Rogers' insistence, he was court-martialed at Crown Point—found guilty and cashiered May 24, 1760. Petitioned Amherst in 1760 for pay from Nov 25, 1759-May 24, 1760. (W.O. 34 100/18.)

_____ **THRIBOUT:** 18th Second Lieutenant
First name unknown.
Service: Lieutenants Wendell's and Wait's winter of 1758-9.
Recruited 23 men for Wait's in May, 1759. (W.O. 34, 54/129.)

GEORGE (JAMES) TURNER: 22nd Second Lieutenant
Entered Corps, Dec 25, 1757, as a Private in J. Stark's.
Promoted to Lieutenant after April 24, 1758, in Moses Brewer's.
Served conspicuously in St. Francis Raid.

CHARLES JOSEPH WALTER: 3rd Second Lieutenant
Sergeant in Hobbs', Aug 1, 1756.
Served at La Barbue Creek with such distinction that he was
promoted to a supernumerary Second Lieutenant in Rogers'
Own on Apr 1, 1757. Resigned Aug 1757.

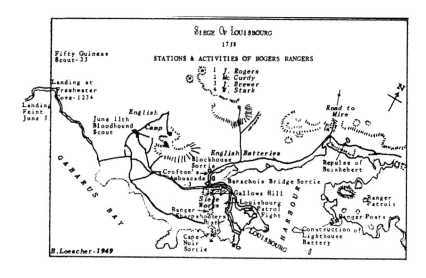

Ensign Carruthers (see p. 47) was killed in his heroic landing at
Freshwater Cove.

THE ENSIGNS

TIMOTHY REED: 21st Ensign
Ensign of W. Stark's, Sept 25, 1759.
Discharged with Company at Boston on Nov 30, 1759.

ELIAS BREWER: 5th Ensign
Of Sudbury, Mass.
Entered March 15, 1757 as a Cadet in J. Stark's. Promoted
in Aug, 1757, to Ensign of the Company. Resigned April 7,
1758, disgruntled because he was not promoted Jan 14, 1758
(paid to April 24, 1758 on roll).

JOHN CALDWELL: 22nd Ensign
Ensign of J. Rogers' Sept 26, 1759. Discharged with
Company at Boston Nov 30, 1759.

ARCHIBALD CAMPBELL, JR.: 14th Ensign
A Scotch Volunteer from the 42nd Highlanders. Son to
Ranger Lieutenant Archibald Campbell, Sr. Served in Rogers'
Cadet Company, Sept 14-Nov 8, 1757. Ensign of Burbank's
after April 7, 1758. Succeeded Duncan Campbell (promoted) as
an Ensign in the 42nd Regiment, July 21, 1758. Lieutenant, Feb
14, 1760.

FRANCIS CARRUTHERS: 12th Ensign
An English Volunteer from the 44th. Served in Rogers'
Cadet Company, Sept 14-Nov 8, 1757. Commissioned Ensign
in J. Rogers' March 30, 1758, replacing Gregory McDonald
killed at Rogers' Rock. Accompanying his Company to
Louisbourg, he was killed June 8, 1758, in his heroic landing at
Freshwater Cove.

RANGER ENSIGN FRANCIS CARRUTHERS Discovers a perilous landing June 8, 1758 for Wolfe's army to besiege Louisbourg. 20x24 oil painting by the author, Burt Loescher.

JOHN CLARK: 13th Ensign
Entered Rogers' Own, April 25, 1757, as a Private.
Sergeant, after Nov 11, 1957. For valor at Rogers' Rock, he was promoted to Ensign of Burbank's (replacing J. White, killed), April 7, 1758. There is no record of his being in the Corps after this date. It is possible that he is the same John Clark who was commissioned Ensign in the 48th, back-dated March 18, 1758. Lieutenant by March 8, 1759.

JONAS ETOWAUKAUM: 10th Ensign
A Stockbridge warrior. Private in Jacob Cheeksaunkun's May 27-Sept 21, 1756. Ensign of Jacob Naunauphtaunk's Feb 6, 1758-Sept 11, 1758. Re-commissioned Ensign, March 25, 1759. Killed and scalped by French Indians, July 28, 1759, at Ticonderoga.

DAVID GILMAN: 20th Ensign
Of Exeter, N.H.
Brother of Ranger Lieutenant Samuel Gilman. Entered Shepherd's as Private on Feb 25, 1758. Left with his brother on April 6, 1758 (resigned). Re-entered Corps in 1759, as Ensign of D. Brewer's. Continued until disbandment, Nov 11, 1760.
In Dec, 1776, he was appointed Colonel of a N.H. Militia Regiment, raised to reinforce the American army in N.Y. In 1777, commissioned Lieutenant in Reid's 2nd N.H. Regiment of Continentals. Served from 1777-1779.

_____ HAZEN: 23rd Ensign
Related to Captain Moses Hazen.
Ensign in his Company by Oct 10, 1759. Discharged with Company Nov 11, 1760.

BENJAMIN HUTCHINGS (HUTCHINS): 18th Ensign
Of Boston, Mass.
Private in Rogers' Own, June 1, 1756-Sept 27, 1756, when he resigned. Re-entered Corps in April, 1759, as Ensign in M.

Brewer's. Resigned during 1759-60 winter when he was promised the Provincial Captaincy of a Company he had raised. He was superceded in the spring by a more senior officer. Expressed his desire to re-enter Rogers' Rangers and Rogers sent him to Amherst at Oswego with dispatches and his recommendation. Amherst re-commissioned him Ensign of Stevens', July 9, 1760. Served until Company was disbanded Nov 11, 1760.

GEORGE KEESER (KEISER): 15th Ensign

Held a brevet as Ensign from Brigadier Lawrence in 1756. After McCormick's capture he succeeded him as Ensign of W. Stark's, about Oct 15, 1758 – to campaign ended at end of year.

JOSHUA MARTIN: 17th Ensign

Of Goffstown, N.H.

Served as a Private, Aug 23-Nov 16, 1754, in Blanchard's scouting Company, guarding the frontiers of the Merrimac River Valley.

Entered Rogers' Rangers as Private in Richard Rogers' Company, Aug 5, 1756.

For valor at La Barbue Creek, Jan 21, 1757, he was promoted to a Sergeancy in Richard Rogers', Feb 24, 1757. Served to Aug 9, 1757, when Company capitulated at Fort William Henry.

Recommended by Rogers on Jan 10, 1758 for the Second Lieutenancy of W. Stark's new Company, but turned down by Loudoun because he was a member of the Fort William Henry capitulation.

Re-entered Corps in 1759 as Ensign of Rogers' Own Company. Second Lieutenant in J. Stark's in 1759, then J. Rogers' in 1760.

During American Revolution he Captained the 28th Militia Company of N.H., from Goffstown, which reinforced Sullivan in Dec, 1775.

He lived to an old age in Goffstown, N.H.

GREGORY McDONALD: 8th Ensign

Entered Rogers' Own Company May 25, 1757, as a Volunteer. Recommended by Rogers on Jan 10, 1758, for the Ensigncy of J. Rogers' new Company. Commissioned same by Loudoun, Jan 14, 1758. Killed at Rogers' Rock March 13, 1758.

EDMUND MUNROE: 26th Ensign

Sergeant-Major of Rogers' Rangers from 1758–March 24, 1760.

Recommended by Rogers May 4, 1760, for Ensigncy of D. Brewer's, but David Gilman superseded him. Received an Ensigncy in Corps before close of 1760.

Disbanded with Corps, Nov 11, 1760.

As a Captain in the Continental Line, he was killed at Monmouth, 1778.

CALEB PAGE, JR.: 2nd Ensign

Of Rumford, and Dunbarton, N.H. Son of the prominent settler of the same name. Companion of the Rogers' brothers in his youth. Entered Richard Rogers' Company, July 24, 1756 as Ensign, but commission was not dated by Loudoun until Aug 29, 1756.

Killed, Jan 21, 1757, at La Barbue Creek.

WILLIAM PEN: 24th Ensign

Entered Corps Nov 24, 1759, as Ensign of Rogers' Own. Served until disbandment of Rogers' Rangers, Nov 11, 1760.

ABRAHAM PERRY: 1st Ensign

Rogers' Original Co. Blanchard's N.H. Regt. Jan-April 25-Nov, 1755 then left service.

Received Captaincy of 2nd Company of Messerve's N.H. Reg. May 1-Nov 21, 1756.

FRANCIS ROLPH: 3rd Ensign

Of Boston, Mass.

Served as a Volunteer in Rogers' Own in late 1756. On Dec 11, 1756 Rogers recommended him for a Ranger Officer's berth. May 20, 1757 commissioned Ensign of Rogers' Own. Resigned Winter 1757-8.

ANDREW ROSS: 7th Ensign

A Scotch Volunteer from the 42nd. Recommended by Rogers Jan 10, 1758 for Ensigncy in a new Company of Rangers. Commissioned by Loudoun Jan 14, 1758. Ensign in Wm. Stark's new Company. Killed March 13, 1758 at Rogers' Rock.

SAMUEL SHEPHERD, JR.: 4th Ensign, Canterbury, N.H.

Served in Ladd's Scouting Company, July 10-Oct 2, 1746 (King George's War).

Entered Rogers' Rangers Feb 15, 1757, as Sergeant in Shepherd's. Ensign after July 24, 1757 (On Nov 14, 1757, roll as Ensign).

Recommended by Rogers on Jan 10, 1758 for First Lieutenancy of J. Brewer's new Company. Crossed out by Loudoun, who left him as Ensign in Shepherd's.

Left service—probably with Captain Shepherd, July 12, 1759.

LAWRENCE SMITH (SMYTH): 9th Ensign

A British Volunteer, recommended and commissioned by Loudoun, Ensign of J. Brewer's new Company, Jan 14, 1758. Probably discharged with Company Nov 30, 1759.

JACOB SKELL: 11th Ensign

Ensign of Wendell's, March 25, 1758. On June 24, 1758 roll.

SAMUEL STARK: 16th Ensign
Born 1726, Londonderry, N.H. Brother of John, William and Archibald.
Entered Corps Oct 5, 1756 as a Private in J. Stark's. Discharged April 15, 1757, refused to serve on 5th establishment.
Re-entered same Company in October or November, 1757. Sick in Hospital on Rogers' Island, Fort Edward, on Nov 24, 1757, roll. Not on April 24, 1758 roll.
An Ensign in the Corps in 1759.
Fell from horse at night during winter of 1759-60. Almost died of exposure before he was discovered. Tendered his resignation to Amherst. Later regretted his resignation and served as a Ranger Volunteer, without pay, in the 1760 campaign, from March 2-Nov 10, 1760 (254 days) "in hopes that a vacancy should offer and he obtain an Ensigncy."
No vacancy occurred, and though Rogers petitioned on his behalf, he was not even paid for his 1760 service, since he was on a volunteer status.
He resided in Derryfield, N.H. Was the second son of Archibald, Sr. Died in 1809.

GIBSON VANELIEU: 27th Ensign
Private in Ogden's to Jan 24, 1762, when Lieutenant Richard Van Tyne was killed. He was promoted to Ensign for valorous conduct in the Battle of Morne Tortenson (filling the Ensign's vacancy as the officers were promoted to fill Van Tyne's vacancy). Vanelieu was not on June 16, 1762 muster at N.Y. when the Company was disbanded.

BENJAMIN WAIT: 25th Ensign
Sergeant in J. Rogers' 1758. In landing at Freshwater Cove at Louisbourg. Ensign of Wait's spring of 1760. Probably left service in spring of 1761. Was not on April 17, 1762 muster at Fort Royal, Martinique.

JAMES WHITE: 6th Ensign

A British Volunteer, recommended and commissioned by Loudoun, Ensign in Bulkeley's Jan 14, 1758. Killed March 13, 1758 at Rogers' Rock.

JOHN WILSON: 19th Ensign

Of Petersham, Mass.

Entered Corps as Private of Rogers' Own March 9, 1757. On Nov 24, 1757 roll.

Ensign in 1759 on Lake George front.

Ensign of J. Rogers' Company in 1760. Discharged with Company Nov 11, 1760.

For extraordinary service commissioned Ensign in the 28th Regiment July 31, 1763.

THE SURGEONS

AMERIAH RUHAMAH CUTTER: 2nd Surgeon
Born at North Yarmouth March 15, 1735. Commissioned May 25, 1757 by Loudoun, "to be Surgeon to the Rangers." Left the Rangers on Oct 10, 1757 for Albany "to recover his health." Carried on Nov 24, 1757 roll (Robert Rogers' Company).
In 1759 he set up shop in Portsmouth, N.H. The following ad appeared in the *New Hampshire Gazette*, No 160, Oct 26, 1759: "To be sold by Ammi Ruhamah Cutter, At his Shop near the State House, Portsmouth - A fresh assortment of Medicines, also spices of all kinds & Painters Colours."

JACOB VEARLAND: 1st Surgeon
From Sept 27, 1756. From Albany, N.Y.

THE ADJUTANT AND PAYMASTER

WILLIAM STEWART: Adjutant

His Memorial to Amherst from Albany, Jan 7, 1760 (W.O. 34, Vol 82, f 6), describes his military service: "Memorial of Adj. Wm. Stewart of the Rangers: ...That he hath been in His Majesty's Service 26 years and 9 months last past. Six years in wars in Flanders. Seven years, Serjeant-Major to 1st Battalion, Royal Americans. The late Brigadier General Forbes made several Proposals to him at New York in 1758 to go with him to the southward, but General Abercrombie told him he intended to provide for him himself and would not permit him to go with the late Forbes.—Your Memorialist therefore humbly prays that your Excellency would be pleased to take his services into Consideration, and he might not be left destitute in a strange land."

While Adjutant to Rogers' Rangers he received 4 shillings sterling per day.

PAUL BURBEEN: Paymaster

Clerk to Rogers' Own Company 1759. Corps Paymaster 1760 (W.O. 34 Vol 82.)

THE CLERKS

ISAAC ANDREW:
Clerk of Jacob Naunauphtaunk's Feb 6, 1758 to end of campaign.

JAMES DEWEY:
Sergeant in Jacob Naunauphtaunk's Feb 6, 1758 to close of campaign. Clerk in Solomon's in 1759.

LAWRENCE EKINS:
Clerk of Moses Brewer's in 1758-9. Deserted in June, 1759. The following was printed in *The Boston Evening Post*, No 1244, July 2, 1759: "Deserted from Capt. Moses Brewer's Company of Rangers, one Lawrence Ekins, formerly belonging to Hanover. He had on when he went away, a Blue Surtout Coat, with brass Buttons, a blue Waistcoat, a pair of Nankeen Breeches, and a dark coloured Wig; is about 22 years of age, and of a midling stature. Whoever takes up and secures said Deserter, and gives Information thereof to Mrs. Elizabeth Brewer at Sudbury, shall receive Twenty Dollars Reward and all necessary Charges paid.

N.B. The said Ekins was Clerk to the above said Captain Brewer, and carried off with him Money and Papers to a very great value."

JOHN McCURDY:
Of Haverhill, Mass.

Lieutenant in 2nd Company of Saltonstall's Massachusetts Regiment in 1756.

Clerk of Rogers' Own Company on June 26, 1757. Discharged Oct 25, 1757.

JOHN WAUWAUMPEQUVNAUNT:
   Clerk of Jacob Cheeksaunkun's Stockbridge Company, May
27, 1756 to ____?
   Loudoun's Order, of Nov 14, 1756, states that
Wauwaumpequvnaunt, had only been out on one scout during
the campaign. When asked to attend for the settling of the
accounts of his company he did not show up. Loudoun
peremptorily ordered that he be struck off the company roll.
(LO 2211.)

THE CADETS

FRANCIS BERNARD:
A Volunteer from the 4th Battalion, Royal Americans. A Cadet in Rogers' Cadet Company Sept 14-Nov 8, 1757. Not commissioned. Petitioned Loudoun in Dec, 1757, that he was returning to Germany and would like to be reimbursed for the Ranger uniform he had to purchase while serving as one of Rogers' Cadets. (LO 5172.)

JOSEPH BOLTON:
A Private in Rogers' Own from June 1, 1756-Feb 24, 1757. Sergeant, Feb 24, 1757. On Roll Nov 24, 1757, as a Volunteer. Not commissioned.

JOHN BOUJOUR:
A Swiss Volunteer from the 4th Battalion, Royal Americans. In Rogers' Cadet Company Sept 14-Nov 8, 1757. Not commissioned.

RICHARD BOYCE:
A British Volunteer from the 48th Regiment. Ranger Cadet, Sept 14-Nov 8, 1757. Not commissioned.

BENJAMIN BRIDGE:
A Ranger Private from Bulkeley's. Entered the Company as a Private on March 12, 1757. Ranger Cadet Sept 14-Nov 8, 1757. Not commissioned.

RONALD CHALMERS:
A British Volunteer unattached to any Regiment. Served with Rogers from Aug, 1756 to April, 1757. Petitioned Loudoun April 5, 1757, from Albany. (LO 3287.) Not commissioned in North America.

JOHN CHRISTOPHER:
A British Volunteer from the 55th. A Ranger Cadet Sept 14-Nov 8, 1757. Ensign in 17th Regiment, March 21, 1758. Lieutenant, Sept 18, 1760.

____ COLLINGWOOD:
A British Volunteer in Eyre's ____ Regiment. Ranger Cadet in Ogden's, June, 1760.

WALTER CROFTON:
English Volunteer 4th King's Own Regiment. Ranger Cadet Sept14-Nov 8 1757. Ensign 46th Regiment Oct 19, 1762.

ANDREW CROTTY
A British Volunteer from the 22nd. He had served as Quartermaster, Ensign, Lieut., in the East Indian Service. A Ranger Cadet Sept 14-Nov 8, 1757. On Nov 19, 1757, he petitioned Loudoun for an Ensigncy in any Regular Corps. (Pargellis, Loudoun *in North America*, p 312. LO 4861.) Commissioned Ensign in the 44th, Sept 15, 1758; Lieutenant Aug 16, 1760. Lieutenant Oct 19, 1762.

LUHAINSANS DEKEFAR:
A Swiss Volunteer from the 4th Battalion Royal Americans. Ranger Cadet, Sept 14-Nov 8, 1757. Not commissioned.

THOMAS DROUGHT:
A British Volunteer from the 44th. Ensign in 80th (Gage's), Dec 25, 1757. Lieutenant July 28, 1758. (Ranger Cadet, Sept 14-Nov 8, 1757).

RICHARD ELRINGTON:
A British Volunteer from the 22nd. Ensign 22nd, July 5, 1758. (Ranger Cadet, Sept 14-Nov 8, 1757).

WILLIAM FRASER:

A Scotch Volunteer from the 42nd Highlanders. Gazetted for an Ensigncy in Gage's 80th, by Barrington, Sept 11, 1757. After serving in Rogers' Cadet Company Sept 14-Nov 8, 1757, he entered Gage's as a Volunteer. (AB 857.) Served until Dec 27, 1757 when he was commissioned Ensign. Lieutenant, Sept 25, 1760.

WILLIAM FRASER, JR:

Son of above. Also a Volunteer in 42nd. Ranger-Cadet, Sept 14-Nov 8, 1757. Ensign in 44th Regiment, March 23, 1758.

____ FRISBOUGH:

A British Volunteer from 2nd Battalion Royal Americans. Not Commissioned. Ranger Cadet from Sept 14-Nov 8, 1757.

ROBERT GIBS:

Entered Rogers' Own Company Aug 20, 1756 as a Ranger Cadet. Not on Feb 24, 1757 roll.

JOHN GRAHAM:

A Scotch Volunteer from 42nd. Ranger Cadet Sept 14-Nov 8, 1757. Ensign 42nd Highlanders, July 25, 1758. Lieutenant July 31, 1760. Captain-Lieutenant Aug 15, 1762.

ALLEN GRANT:

A British Volunteer from 2nd Battalion Royal Americans. Served as a Volunteer for two years before he petitioned Loudoun on Feb 3, 1758 for an officer's berth. (LO 5532.) Ranger Cadet Sept 14-Nov 8, 1757. Commissioned Ensign in the 60th Royal Americans on July 28, 1758. Lieutenant Oct 7, 1763.

Two ROGERS' RANGERS listen with interest to Ranger Luxford Goodwin, the 'Aesop' of Rogers' Rangers. Harper's Magazine.

THE SERGEANTS

JAMES ARCHIBALD: Of Rogers' Own Company.
A Sergeant, Sept 22 to Dec 13, 1755 in Capt. J. Todd's 3rd Co. of Gilman's N.H. Provincial Regiment. Sergeant, Rogers' Own, Nov 25, 1755 until April 12, 1756 when he was captured and taken to Montreal. Escaped in Sept, 1756. Re-entered Rogers' Own on Sept 26, 1756 as Sergeant. Not on Feb 24, 1757 roll.

ISAAC BALDWIN (BALMDING): Of J. Stark's.
Entered March 8, 1757, as Private. On April 24, 1758 roll.

JAMES BALLARD: Of J. Stark's.
Entered J. Stark's Jan 18, 1758 as Private. Promoted to Sergeant March 13, 1758, succeeding one of two Sergeants of Stark's Company killed at Rogers' Rock.

JONATHAN BARNES: Of Rogers' Own.
Feb 24-Aug 24, 1757. Died of Smallpox between Aug 24 and Sept 2, 1757.

BEAU DE BIEN ("BEAUBIEN") Of William Stark's.
Captain William Stark's Wolf-dog carried on his roll as a Sergeant drawing pay and rations for him. Stark found the dog while on a hunting trip north. A French officer was beating the dog and Stark intervened. A fierce duel ensued between Stark and the big Frenchman, in which Stark came out on top. The dog gladly attached himself to his newfound champion. Stark named him Sergeant Beau de Bien but it was shortened by the Rangers to "Beaubien," while he was most generally known as "The Sergeant." He lived to a ripe old age, and though he never boasted of his deeds, he was deemed quite a hero. (G. Waldo Browne, Bits of Biography in *With Rogers' Rangers*, pp 278-286.)

SAMUEL BEEMAN: Of David Brewer's.
Enlisted Jan 1, 1760 as Sergeant.

THOMAS BEVERLY: Of Rogers' Own.
Captured Feb 12, 1760 at the Ranger Payroll Massacre.
Loaned 24 livres by Tute while a prisoner at Montreal. While at
Montreal became friendly with Governor Vaudreuil and lived
at his house. Escaped on April 27, 1760. Arrived at Crown
Point on May 4, 1760.

WILLIAM BEVERLY: Of Shepherd's (Tute's).
Entered Feb 18, 1757 as a Sergeant. Demoted to Private after
the "Whipping Post Mutiny" in 1757. Re-instated to Sergeant
sometime after April 24, 1758 and served conspicuously until
the end of the war.

OLIVER BATES: Of Bulkeley's.
Entered March 15, 1757. On Nov 24, 1757 roll.

JOHN BOLTON (BOTTON): Of Shepherd's.
Entered Sept 25, 1757. Sergeant Feb 25, 1758. In LaCorne's
Ambuscade.

JOSEPH BOLTON: Of James Rogers'.
Entered as Sergeant, March 12, 1760.

SANDERS BRADBURY: Of M. Hazen's.
Of Haverhill, Mass.
Served with Butler at Fort Miamis in 1760-61. Discharged at
N.Y., Jan 24, 1762.

BENJAMIN BRADLEY: Of Concord, N.H.
See Vol. II, and Index.

JASON BREWER: Of J. Brewer's.
Entered as Sergeant, March 17, 1760.

NATH BRYANT: Of D. Brewer's.
Enlisted as Sergeant, March 10, 1760.

THOMAS BUCK: Of Ogden's.
Served in West Indies, 1761-62.
Discharged about June 16, 1762.

GEORGE BUFORD: Of Ogden's.
Served in West Indies, 1761-62.
Discharged about June 16, 1762.

NATHANIEL (OR CALEB) BURBANK: ____

JONAS BUTTERFIELD: Of J. Rogers'.
Entered as Sergeant, April 21, 1760.

ROBERT CAHOON: Of Ogden's.
Served in West Indies, 1761-2.
Discharged about June 16, 1762.

SAMUEL CAHOON (CALHOUN): Of J. Stark's.
Entered March 1, 1758. Promoted to Sergeant March 13, 1758 (succeeding Jacob Townsend, killed at Rogers' Rock).

JOHN CASTLEMAN: Of Wendell's.
Sergeant Feb 6, 1758 roll. On June 24, roll.

WILLIAM CLARK: Of Rogers' Own.
Entered as Sergeant, March 9, 1757. On Nov 24, 1757 roll. Re-enlisted Feb 24, 1760, as a Private. Re-instated to his Sergeantcy on March 24, 1760. Discharged Oct 25, 1760, at Crown Point. Walked home by way of No. 4, N.H.

EPHRAIM CLEAVELAND: Of Wait's.
In Detroit Expedition 1760.

JOHN CRAIGE:
Entered in Oct, 1757. Enlisted by Lt. James Rogers as a Private. Sick present, on Nov 24, 1757 roll. Served as Sergeant in Wait's in West Indies, 1761-2. Discharged with Company about June 16, 1762.

JOHN DAVIS: Of Wendell's.
Sergeant, April 1, 1758. On June 24 roll.

ELIJAH DENBOW: Of J. Brewer's.
Entered as Sergeant, March 16, 1760.

JOHN DINSMORE: Of Bulkeley's.
Entered April 25, 1757. On Nov 24, 1757 roll.

ZEBULON (LEMUEL) DREW: Of Shepherd's.
Entered Feb 15, 1757. Demoted to Private apparently after "Whipping Post Mutiny." Reported dead on Nov 19, 1757, probably of smallpox at Fort Edward.

JOHN EVANS: Of Richard Rogers' and J. Rogers'.
Entered Aug 5, 1756 as a Private. Promoted to Sergeant, Feb 24, 1757. Served in that capacity until Company disbanded Aug 24, 1757. (In St. Francis Raid?) Re-entered as Sergeant of J. Rogers', March 27, 1760. Discharged Oct 25, 1760 at Crown Point. Marched home by way of No. 4, N.H.

TIMOTHY FARNHAM: Of M. Hazen's.
Of Haverhill, Mass. Served with Butler at Fort Miamis 1760-61. Discharged at N.Y., Jan 24, 1762.

ABEL FARRER (FERROR): Of Shepherd's.
Entered Feb 17, 1757. Sergeant by Sept 25, 1757. Sick in camp on Nov 24, 1757. Demoted to Private between Nov 24, 1757 and Feb 25, 1758. Discharged, or died by April 9, 1758.

BENONI FARRON: Of J. Brewer's.
Entered as Sergeant March 14, 1760.

BENJAMIN FERRIN: Of J. Stark's.
Entered after Jan 14, 1758, as a Sergeant. Apparently a friend of J. Stark's for he superseded all veteran Privates by entering the Corps at this late date as a Sergeant. On April 24, 1758 roll.

PHILIP FLANDERS: Of J. Stark's.
Entered March 1, 1757. Sick present, Nov 24, 1757. Promoted to Sergeant after Jan 14, 1757. Killed at Rogers' Rock March 13, 1758.

EBNER FOWLER: Of Richard Rogers'.
Of Rumford N.H. Entered Aug 4, 1756. Discharged Nov 1, 1756.

ABNER FRENCH: Of Wait's.
Served in West Indies 1761-62. Discharged with disbanded company about June 16, 1762.

_____ GEER:
Connecticut Provincial Sergeant enlisted in Rogers' Rangers Feb 15, 1758 at Rogers' Island.

LUXFORD GOODWIN: Of Stevens'.
Sergeant about Sept, 1760. Discharged at Crown Point, Oct 25, 1760. Walked home by way of No. 4, N.H.
Born in Rumford, N.H., Goodwin was an outstanding Ranger Sergeant in 1760. He was one of four volunteer Rangers to carry vital dispatches from Amherst to Murray in Quebec. After many odysseys they arrived and returned to Amherst with dispatches. On Aug 30, he petitioned for the tenure of duty as King's Ferryman above Number Four, N.H. on the road to Crown Point. Which office, he apparently acquired. (W.O. 34, Vol 200, ff 47-8, Vol 51, ff 198.)

Facsimile of Ranger Sergt. James Hackett's role in building
Amherst's Lake Champlain Fleet in 1759, by R. F. Heinrich.
Courtesy National Life Ins. Vt.

DANIEL GREENOUGH: Of Hazen's.

Entered Corps as Private in Richard Rogers', April 1, 1757. Served until Company disbanded Aug 24, 1757. Re-entered Corps in Jan or Feb, 1758, as a Sergeant in John McCurdy's new Company (later Hazen's).

Served at Siege and Massacre of Fort William Henry; in Siege of Louisbourg; in Lt. Hazen's St. Anne winter raid from Fort Frederic, N.S. in 1759. In various actions and scouts preceding fall of Quebec. In Lt. Butler's attempt to journey to Amherst via Maine with dispatches. In Lt. Montressor's successful mission from Quebec to Maine with the dispatches in Jan-Feb, 1760, one of the most arduous marches of the war, rivaling Rogers' St. Francis Raid retreat in hardships suffered.

THOMAS GROVER (GLOVER): Of Rogers' Own.

Of Worcester, Mass. Entered March 10, 1757 as a Private in J. Stark's. Still in Company by April 24, 1758.

Sergeant of Rogers' Own by May 1, 1759.

Deserted May 31, 1759. A $30.00 reward offered in August for his arrest. "...A lusty stout man 6 feet high..."

JAMES HACKETT: Of J. Stark's.

Reported as a Sergeant in July, 1758. Sergeant in 1759. Captured with Fletcher in his battle near St. John's and La Prairie on Aug 27, 1759. Remained a prisoner at Montreal until exchanged Nov 15, 1759.

Served until disbandment of Rangers Nov 11, 1760. In American Revolution he was appointed to Lt.-Col. of Wingate's Regt, July 4, 1776, but his services as a ship-builder were needed more to create our first little navy. As Master-Builder he was instrumental in fitting out and creating the *McClary, Hampden, Raleigh* and the *America* taking time out only to serve at Saratoga in Langdon's N.H. Independent Company. For his indispensable service Hackett was brevetted a Colonel and commanded a battalion of artillery of three companies at Portsmouth. He had the honor of receiving General

Washington with a "great salute" on the occasion of his reception at Portsmouth, Oct 31, 1789.

JOSIAH HALE (HALD): Of Shepherd's.
Entered Feb 17, 1757, as a Private. Sergeant on Sept 25, 1757 roll. Killed March 13, 1758 at Rogers' Rock. 1/4/9 ½ d pay due.

BENJAMIN HALL: Of Shepherd's.
Feb 16, 1757. Nov 24, sick in New England. Sergeant by Feb 25, 1758 to ____?

PARTRIDGE HAMILTON: Of Rogers' Own.
Private June 1, 1756, Sergeant July 24, 1757. In service Nov 1757.

SAMUEL HAMILTON: Of Rogers' Own.
Private Feb 25, 1757 to ____ 1757. Sergeant Nov 24, 1757 to ____?

LOPHER HEDDY: Of Ogden's.
Served in West Indies 1761-62. Discharged about June 16, 1762.

JAMES HENRY: Of Rogers' Own and Richard Rogers'.
An original Rogers' Ranger. A Private of Rogers' Company, Blanchard's N.H. Regt. Served in 1st, 2nd and 3rd establishments of Rogers' Own Company. Entered 4th establishment June 1, 1756. Promoted to Sergeant July 23, 1756. Captured at La Barbue Creek Jan 21, 1757. Escaped. Recommended by Rogers, Dec 11, 1756 for an officer's berth in the ranging service. Re-entered the Corps as a Private in Richard Rogers' Company, Feb 24, 1757.

HENRY HILL: Of Shepherd's. Entered Feb 15, 1757. On Nov 24, 1757 roll as a Private. Discharged same day as unfit for duty. Not on Feb 25, 1758 roll. Although a Sergeant, exact tenure is not known.

WILLIAM HOLDEN: Of Richard Rogers'. Entered Aug 2, 1756 as a Private. Promoted to Sergeant, Feb 24, 1757. Served until Company disbanded Aug 24, 1757.

____ HOLMES: Of Rogers' Own. Enlisted 17 recruits for Rogers in April 1760.

JOSEPH HOPKINS: Sergeant-Major of Rogers' Rangers in 1759.

JONATHAN HOWARD: Of Hobbs'. Entered Aug 1, 1756 at Boston. Killed Jan 21, 1757, at La Barbue Creek.

STEPHEN HOYT (HOIT): Of Rogers' Own. From June 1, 1756 to April 15, 1757. Refused sixth establishment at less pay. Dies in St. Francis Raid.

ASHBOLL HUMPHRIES: Of Richard Rogers'. Entered Feb 24, 1757 as Sergeant. Served until Aug 24, 1757 - Company was disbanded.

WILLIAM HUTCHINS: Of J. Stark's. Entered Jan 13, 1758, as Private. Sergeant by May 1, 1759. Deserted May 31, 1759. $30.00 reward offered in August for his arrest: "...A lusty stout man 6 feet high..." Hutchins was from Harvard, Mass.

ROBERT JACQUIS: Of Wait's. Served in West Indies 1761-2. Discharged about June 16, 1762.

MOSES KELSEY: Of Shepherd's.
Entered Feb 15, 1757. On Nov 24, 1757. Recruited in New England for Shepherd's. Killed March 13, 1758 at Rogers' Rock. 1/4/9 ½ d pay due.

ANDREW KILSON: Of Rogers' Own.
Private Feb 24 to Nov 1757. Sergeant Nov 24, 1757 to ____?

JOSEPH KOONEHAUNT: Stockbridge Sergt.
In Jacob C. and Solomon U. Companies from March to dischargement Oct 28, 1759.

JOSEPH LAIN: Of J. Stark's.
Entered after Jan 14, 1758 as Sergeant.
Apparently a friend of Stark's for he superseded all veteran Privates by entering the Corps at this late date as a Sergeant. On April 24, 1758 roll.

JOB LIBBY: Of Shepherd's.
Entered Feb 17, 1757. Not on Nov, 1757 roll.

THOMAS LORD: Of Speakman's.
Entered Aug 1, 1756 at Boston. In service Nov 24, 1757.

JOSIAH LOWNSBURY: Of Rogers' Own.
Private June 1, 1756. Sergeant Feb 24, 1757 to ____?

THOMPSON MAXWELL:
Private and Sergeant of David Brewer's, 1759 and 1760.

WILLIAM McCLENNING: Of Hobbs'.
Entered Aug 1, 1756 at Boston as a Private. On furlough Dec 14, 1756. Sergeant Feb 24, 1757. Does not appear after March 24, 1757.

_____ McCULLOUGH: Of Rogers' Own.
Evidently left the service on March 24, 1760.

JOSEPH McCRACKEN (McCRACKON, McCRAKING McCRECKEN): Of Rogers' Own.
Of Worcester, Mass. Entered J. Stark's as a Private March 11, 1757. Sick present Nov 24, 1757. In service April 14, 1758 to ? Sergeant Rogers' Own by May 1, 1759. Deserted May 31, 1759. $30 reward offered in August for his arrest... "a lusty, stout man, 6 feet high..."

RANAL McDANIEL: Of Wendell's.
Sergeant April 7, 1758 to June 24, to ?

PETER McINTIRE (McINTYRE): Of Wait's.
Entered Feb 25, 1758, as Private in J. Stark's. In Rogers' Own, by Nov, 1759. Captured with Captain Tute, March 31, 1760. Loaned 112 livres by Tute while a prisoner at Montreal. Served as Sergeant in Wait's in West Indies 1761-2. Discharged about June 16, 1762.

_____ McKANE: Of Shepherd's (Tute's).
Captured in La Gallette Mission Sept 22, 1759. Exchanged Nov 15, 1759.

JAMES McNEIL: Of Rogers' Own.
Entered as Corporal Nov 5, 1755 to April 1, 1756. Private June 1, 1756 to Feb 24, 1758. Sergeant Feb 24-July 24, 1757. Died?

JOHN MITCHELL: of Rogers' Own.
Of Londonderry, N.H. Saddler. Marched from Ipswich. Captured April 12, 1755(?). He died in France before Feb 16, 1758.

WILLIAM MOORE: Of Rogers' Own.
Of Stratham, N.H. Private April 25, 1757. Sergeant about Dec 1758.

DAVID MURRAY: Of D. Brewer's.
Enlisted as Sergeant, March 2, 1760.

JAMES OSGOOD: Of Rogers' Own.
Private March 24, 1757 to Nov 24, 1757. Re-enlisted Feb 20, 1760 as Private. Promoted to Sergeant March 24, 1760.

WILLIAM PARKER: Of Ogden's.
Served in West Indies 1761-2. Discharged about June 16, 1762.

ROBERT PARNELL: Of Rogers' Own.
Private March 11, 1757. Sergeant about Nov 24, 1757. Killed March 13, 1758 at Rogers' Rock.

_____ PHILLIP: (Stockbridge)
Sergeant 1759-?

WILLIAM RANSON: Of Shepherd's.
Entered Sept 25, 1757. Sergeant about Nov, 1757. On Feb 24-April 24, 1758 rolls as Private.

ALEXANDER ROBB: Of Bulkeley's.
Entered Feb 24, 1757. Sergeant by April 25, 1757. In service Nov 24, 1757.

JOHN ROSSIER: Of Rogers' Own.
Private Feb 24-Nov 24, 1757, etc. Sergeant?

TRISTRUM SANBORN (SAMBORN): Of Shepherd's.
Entered Feb 22, 1757. Sergeant Feb 25-April 24, 1758 to ____?

JOHN SEAGRAVES: Of Shepherd's.
Entered Feb 25, 1758. In service April, 1758.

JACOB SEVER: Of Wendell's.
Sergeant, Feb 15-June 24, 1758, to ____?

MARTIN SEVERANCE: Of Rogers' Own.
Born at Deerfield, Mass. 41 years old in 1759. Light complexion. Private March 9, to after July 24, 1757. Sergeant by Nov 24, 1757. Captured with Stevens and Stone at Lake George Narrows June 25, 1758. Sent to Quebec and exchanged to England. Signed on *HMS Essex* as a seaman in order to gain passage back to N.Y. Upon arriving, the ship's Captain, John Curtin refused to relinquish him. Upon Major Rogers' intercession he was released to re-join the Corps about May 11, 1759.

MATTHEW SEVERANCE: Of Burbank's.
From Deerfield, Mass. Nephew of Martin Severance. Deserted July 13, 1759. $30 reward offered the day of his desertion by Lt. McMullen.

NATHAN SIMONDS: Of Hobbs' (Bulkeley's).
Entered Aug 1, 1756 at Boston as Sergeant. At work at Fort Edward on Dec 14, 1756 roll. Discharged May 30, 1757. There is apparently a discrepancy on the June 24-Aug 24, 1757 roll for he is carried on this muster. Either that or he re-enlisted between May 30 and June 24, 1757. This would account for his being in service Nov 24, 1757. Demoted to Private March 21, 1757. Re-enlisted same day as Private.

BRYAN SWEENY: Of J. Stark's.
Entered Feb 24, 1757 as a Sergeant. Private by May 25, 1757. In service April 24, 1758 as Private.

JACOB TOWNSEND: Of J. Stark's.
Entered Aug 1, 1756 at Boston as a Corporal in Speakman's.
Became a Private when Company went on 5th establishment.
Sergeant by Nov 24, 1757 in J. Stark's. Killed March 13, 1758 at
Rogers' Rock.

ROBERT TRUETT: Of Speakman's.
Entered Aug 1, 1756 at Boston as Sergeant. Reported killed
Jan 21, 1757 at La Barbue Creek. Recruiting by March 24, 1757.
Apparently was not successful as a recruiter for he is a Private
on the April 24, 1757 roll. July 24, 1757 last mention.

JASON WAIT: Of J. Rogers'.
Entered as Sergeant April 1, 1760.

JAMES WARREN: Of Bulkeley's.
Entered March 15, 1757 as Sergeant to Nov 24, 1757 to
____?

HENDRICK WAUPUNKSCOT: Of Jacob C.
From May 27-Nov 11, 1756.

____ WELLESLEY: Of Burbank's?

PHILLIP WELLS: Of Rogers' Own.
Private Nov 26, 1755 to Sergeantcy by Nov 24, 1757. In
service as Sergeant on July 23, 1759.

BENJAMIN WILLIAMS: Of J. Brewer's.
Entered as Sergeant March 26, 1760.

ANDREW WILSON:
Mentioned as a 1759 Sergeant.

ABRAHAM WNAUMPOS: Of Jacob N.
From March 1759. Captured with Capt. Jacob N. in St.
Francis mission Aug 8, 1759. Exchanged Nov 8, 1759.

THE CORPORALS

JOHN EDMUNDS: Of Hobbs'.
From Oct 24, 1756 until killed Jan 21, 1757.

SAMUEL FISK: Of Speakman's.
At Boston Aug 1, 1756 until killed Jan 21, 1757 La Barbue Creek.

NATHANIEL JOHNSON: Of Rogers' Own.
Nov 5, 1755-Jan 4, 1756.

PHINEAS PARKER: Of Speakman's.
At Boston Aug 1, 1757. Discharged: May 31, 1757, refused 5th establishment. Had been promoted Corporal Feb 24, 1757 replacing Samuel Fisk killed Jan 21, 1757.

EBENEZER PERRY: Of Hobbs'.
At Boston Aug 1, 1756. At work Fort Edward Dec 14, 1756. Shoulder wound Battle La Barbue Creek. Refused 5th establishment May 1757.

JOHN ROBERTSON: Of Hobbs'.
Aug 1, 1756 at Boston. Oct 24, 1756 demoted to Private. Reinstated Corporal by Feb 24, 1757 replacing a Corporal killed Jan 21, 1757 but quickly reduced to Private when Loudoun's 5th establishment abolished Corporals in Rogers' Rangers. Killed May 11, 1757 with 16 days pay due. (LO 6645 [1].)

WILLIAM SWAN: Of Shepherd's.
Aug 1, 1756 at Boston as Speakman's Corporal. Private Feb 24, 1757 when Company became J. Stark's and Corporals eliminated by 5th establishment (see above). Discharged May 31, 1757 refused terms.

EPHRAIM WHEELER: Of Hobbs'.
Aug 1, 1756 at Boston. Discharged May 30, 1757 refused 5th establishment.

INDEX

Rank is shown in parentheses. To facilitate use of this index, individual Rangers with the same surname are given separate entries, while non-Rangers, such as spouses and parents with a common surname are grouped in the same entry.

Lightning Source UK Ltd.
Milton Keynes UK
UKOW032243010713

213091UK00016B/1075/P